W9-CZS-597

★ ★ ★ ★

THE NEW BOOK OF KNOWLEDGE

PRESENTS

HISTORIC U.S. MONUMENTS

★ ★ ★ ★

Compilation Copyright © 2005 by Scholastic, Inc.
Arlington National Cemetery © 1995 by Children's Press®, Inc.
The Capitol © 1995 by Children's Press®, Inc.
Ellis Island © 2005 by Judith Jango-Cohen
Mount Rushmore © 1999 by Children's Press®, Inc.
The Statue of Liberty © 2004 by Elaine Landau
The Tomb of the Unknown Soldier © 2003 by Children's Press, a Division of Scholastic Inc.
The Vietnam Memorial © 2003 by Children's Press, a Division of Scholastic Inc.
The Washington Monument © 2004 by Elaine Landau

All rights reserved. Published by Scholastic Inc.
No part of this publication may be reproduced in whole or in part, or stored in a retrieval system, or
transmitted in any form or by any means, electronic, mechanical, photocopying, recording, or otherwise,
without written permission of the publisher.
For information regarding permission, write to: Scholastic Inc.,
Attention: Permissions Department, 557 Broadway, New York, NY 10012.

Published by Scholastic Inc.
90 Old Sherman Turnpike, Danbury, CT 06816.

SCHOLASTIC and associated logos are trademarks and/or registered trademarks of Scholastic Inc.

ISBN 0-7172-8633-9
Printed in the U.S.A.
First Printing, October 2005

★ ★ ★ ★

THE NEW BOOK OF KNOWLEDGE

PRESENTS

HISTORIC U.S. MONUMENTS

IMPORTANT MONUMENTS OF THE UNITED STATES

SCHOLASTIC INC.

New York   Toronto   London   Auckland   Sydney
Mexico City   New Delhi   Hong Kong   Buenos Aires

CONTRIBUTORS

De Capua, Sarah
The Vietnam Memorial

Jango-Cohen, Judith
Ellis Island

Landau, Elaine
The Statue of Liberty
The Washington Monument

Santella, Andrew
The Capitol
Mount Rushmore

Stein, R. Conrad
Arlington National Cemetery

Wachtel, Roger
The Tomb of the Unknown Soldier

CONTENTS

★ ★ ★ ★

Chapter 1

Arlington National Cemetery

R. Conrad Stein

For U.S. Marines, the February 1945 assault on Iwo Jima was the bloodiest battle of World War II. Japanese troops defending the tiny island fought with a desperate fury that shocked even those Marines who were veterans of other Pacific battles. After four days of savage combat on Iwo Jima, a group of Marines reached the top of Mount Suribachi, Iwo Jima's highest point. Amid the smoke and roar of battle, six men raised an American flag on a tall pole while a photographer named Joe Rosenthal snapped a picture. That picture inspired Americans at home and became the most famous photograph taken during World War II.

Joe Rosenthal's famous photograph of Marines raising the American flag at Iwo Jima

Ira Hayes

The U.S. Marine Corps War Memorial reproduces the Joe Rosenthal Iwo Jima photograph. The memorial is near Arlington National Cemetery.

One of the Mount Suribachi flag raisers was twenty-two-year-old Ira Hayes. He was a Pima Indian, born on a reservation in Arizona. After fighting at Iwo Jima, Hayes returned to the United States a war hero. A painfully shy man, Hayes could not adjust to his sudden fame. One night in 1955 he got drunk, passed out, and died. Ira Hayes now rests at the Arlington National Cemetery in Arlington, Virginia. Some people who knew him believe that finally, in the quiet grounds of the cemetery, he found peace. Two other men who were in the historic picture—Rene Gagnon and Michael Strank —also rest at Arlington.

Joe Louis worked to raise soldier morale during World War II with his boxing exhibitions. He was a hero to many African Americans.

Joe Louis was not a war hero, but during the 1930s and 1940s, he was almost as famous as the president of the United States. Louis was the boxing heavyweight champion of the world from 1937 to 1949. Nicknamed "the Brown Bomber," he had a lightning-quick left hand and a thunderous right. Many experts still say he was the best prizefighter in history. An African American, he was especially idolized by the nation's blacks.

Joe Louis's gravesite at Arlington

Shortly after the U.S. entered World War II, Joe Louis enlisted in the army as a private. He traveled from camp to camp giving boxing exhibitions to soldiers, thereby helping to improve morale. Some people criticized Joe Louis's efforts. In the 1940s, African Americans in many states were not allowed in the same movie theaters, restaurants, or public schools as whites. Even the army in which Louis served was segregated, with blacks and whites kept in

★ ★ ★ ★

separate units. A critic once asked Louis why he was willing to help a nation that treated his people so poorly. Louis answered, "I don't think Mr. Hitler would do any better." Joe Louis died in 1981, and he now rests at Arlington National Cemetery, where there is no segregation.

There are more than 250,000 graves at Arlington. Fully three-quarters of them are marked by simple, government-issued headstones, which are curved at the top and rise about knee-high to the average man. Seemingly endless rows of these white headstones stretch over rolling acres at Arlington. The rows resemble soldiers standing at attention. Though most of the gravestones are identical, each represents the life of a man or a woman and consequently tells an individual, and often heroic, story.

There are more than 250,000 graves at Arlington National Cemetery.

Arlington is one of 114 national cemeteries maintained by the United States government. The major purpose of a national cemetery is to serve as a burial place for veterans of the country's armed forces. Situated across the Potomac River from Washington, D.C., Arlington has long been close to many Americans' hearts. It is the final home of citizens from all backgrounds. Buried there are ex-presidents as well as former slaves. More than four million people visit the cemetery every year. A walk over its grassy hills is a walk through American history.

*Mary Ann
Randolph Custis*

The land we now know as Arlington National Cemetery was purchased in 1778 by John Parke Custis. Mr. Custis had a famous mother—Martha Washington, wife of the nation's first president. John Custis was Martha Washington's son by her first marriage. Custis died while serving in George Washington's army in the Revolutionary War. After he died, the land was passed on to his son, George Washington Parke Custis.

The younger Custis named the land Arlington, after a family estate that once stood on the Virginia shore. He married and raised a beautiful daughter, Mary Ann Randolph Custis. The family lived in a mansion, called Arlington House, which was built on the property's highest hill.

*George Washington
Parke Custis,
Martha
Washington's
grandson*

Robert E. Lee (1807–1870) was commander of the Confederate Army through most of the Civil War. Lee's Virginia plantation eventually became Arlington National Cemetery.

In 1831, Mary Ann married a young army lieutenant, Robert E. Lee. The marriage brought another Virginia family, as old and as honored as the Washingtons, into the Arlington story. Lee's father was "Light Horse Harry" Lee, a dashing commander who led a cavalry unit in the Revolutionary War. For almost thirty years, Robert E. Lee and his wife, Mary Ann, lived happily on the Arlington plantation, which then spread over 1,100 acres.

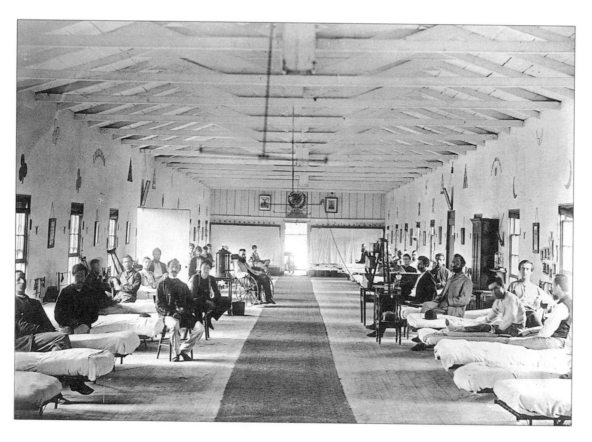

A Washington, D.C., hospital during the Civil War

In 1861, the Lee family and the nation were ripped apart by the Civil War. The South's desire to continue owning slaves was the root cause of the terrible war. It raged for four years and cost more lives than any other conflict in American history.

Though he was a southerner, Robert E. Lee hated slavery. He once wrote, "Slavery is a moral and political evil in any society, a greater evil to the white man than to the black." Still, Lee felt deep emotional ties to Virginia and to the southern states. He left his home and his family to command the Confederate Army. Lee never again returned to Arlington, the home he loved.

President Lincoln (center) and Union officers

Throughout the Civil War, Arlington was in the hands of Union (northern) troops. Just across the Potomac River from Arlington, the city of Washington served as an immense Union Army camp.

At the height of the conflict, some two thousand wounded and ill Union soldiers were shipped each week from battlegrounds to hospitals in the nation's capital. Many of those stricken troops died. Nearby graveyards quickly became full. So in the spring of 1864, President Abraham Lincoln asked Quartermaster General Montgomery Meigs to establish a new national cemetery. Meigs selected Arlington as the site.

Montgomery Meigs

* * * *

A Civil War memorial at Arlington National Cemetery

Many historians believe that Meigs, who despised Robert E. Lee, chose Arlington just to deprive the Lee family of its estate. In a cruel irony of war, Meigs's own son, Lieutenant John Rodgers Meigs, was killed in action in October 1864. He was buried in what was once Mrs. Lee's rose garden.

When the Civil War ended in 1865, there were already 18,000 graves at Arlington. Many of the dead belonged to the South's defeated Confederate Army. Today, the old Confederate grave sites are easy to pick out because they have pointed, rather than curved, stones. An Arlington legend says the stones were designed by southerners with points on top to prevent Yankees (northerners) from sitting on them.

Confederate soldiers' gravestones in Arlington have pointed, not curved, tops.

Arlington soon became the nation's most prestigious military cemetery. The remains of some soldiers who fought in previous wars were moved from other cemeteries and re-buried at Arlington. The cemetery now holds veterans of all American wars from the American Revolution of the 1700s to the Persian Gulf War of 1992. Some of the honored dead at Arlington were generals or admirals whose deaths commanded newspaper headlines. Others were common soldiers who fell on the battlefield, their deaths unnoticed by anyone except their families and friends.

More than four million people visit Arlington every year.

John Clem

Oliver Wendell Holmes

One grave holds John Clem, a Civil War veteran known as the "Drummer Boy of Chickamauga." Clem ran away from home at age ten and served as a drummer boy for the Union. After the war, he stayed in the army and climbed to the rank of brigadier general. At age sixty-five, Clem tried to re-enlist so he could fight in World War I, but he was turned down because he was too old.

Another Civil War soldier resting at Arlington is Oliver Wendell Holmes. His fame came not on the battlefield, but later, as one of the greatest justices ever to serve on the United States Supreme Court. As a young army officer, Holmes was fighting in a battle near Washington when he noticed that this skirmish had a famous observer. Standing tall above a rampart was President Abraham Lincoln, who watched the combat while bullets whistled dangerously close to his head. Holmes cried out, "Get down, you fool!" Finally, Lincoln ducked. He later said to Holmes, "Young man, I'm glad you know how to talk to a civilian."

Abner Doubleday is also buried at Arlington. Doubleday was the Union general in charge of Fort Sumter when it was fired upon by Confederate ships. But Doubleday's claim to fame is that for generations, he was believed to be the inventor of baseball. This event was supposed to have happened at Cooperstown,

New York, in 1839, when Doubleday was a cadet in training at the nearby West Point Military Academy. More than a century later, baseball experts have proven this story to be a myth.

Historians believe the Spanish-American War, fought in 1898, helped to ease the bitterness that inflamed the country during the great Civil War. In the brief Spanish-American War, men of the northern and the southern states fought side by side, displaying a harmony that surprised their fathers, who still remembered the past conflict. A monument honoring Spanish-American War veterans was erected at Arlington in 1902. The monument was dedicated by that conflict's most celebrated veteran—President Theodore Roosevelt. Another memorial stands at Arlington honoring the many American women who served as nurses and died in the Spanish-American War.

Abner Doubleday

Theodore Roosevelt (center, raised sword) was a military hero in the Spanish-American War. He later became president.

John J. Pershing

Few conflicts in history were as terrible as World War I, in which poison gas, machine guns, and rapid-fire artillery killed infantrymen in ghastly numbers. Commanding the American forces in that conflict was John J. Pershing. After the United States and its allies claimed victory in the war, a grateful Congress gave Pershing the title General of the Armies. It was a rank so rare that it had been held previously only by George Washington. Some people whispered that Pershing, though a splendid leader, was also an arrogant man who was unable to talk to his troops. But before he died in 1948, he requested his grave at Arlington be marked with a simple, government-issued stone, and that he be buried in a spot surrounded by the common soldiers he had commanded. In a grave near General Pershing's, his grandson is buried—Lt. Richard Pershing was killed in Vietnam in 1968.

America entered World War II when the Japanese bombed Pearl Harbor, Hawaii, on

General Pershing's burial ceremony at Arlington

Audie Murphy

December 7, 1941. Just four months after that attack, Jimmie Doolittle, who now lies at Arlington, led a flight of sixteen two-engine bombers on a daring raid against Japan. The huge planes had to take off from the pitching deck of an aircraft carrier in the middle of the Pacific Ocean and fly hundreds of miles over enemy-held waters to their target. For his bravery, Doolittle won the Congressional Medal of Honor, the nation's highest award.

The most decorated American soldier of World War II was a baby-faced Texas farm boy named Audie Murphy. Firing a machine gun mounted on a burned-out tank, Murphy once stopped an attack by some 250 German infantrymen. Though he was hailed as the nation's bravest soldier, the army was not Murphy's first choice. He had tried to enlist in the Marines, but he was turned down because he was too short. In 1971, Murphy was killed in an airplane crash and was buried at Arlington.

World War II hero Jimmie Doolittle, who is buried at Arlington

Marguerite Higgins was a news reporter who covered the Korean War. She is considered one of the most important American journalists of the century.

The Korean War of 1950–53 is often called the "Forgotten War." While it was being fought, it was largely ignored by the people at home, and it was later given scant mention in most history books. Reporting on the war for *Life* magazine was correspondent Marguerite Higgins, the only female correspondent near the front when the war began. Higgins's important role in the war was alerting the army and the public to the fact that the American soldiers' antitank weapons were outdated and ineffective against the giant North Korean tanks. Higgins now rests at Arlington. Korean War veterans hail her as a lone voice reminding Americans of the Forgotten War raging in a faraway land.

＊　　＊　　＊　　＊

Not since the Civil War has a conflict divided the nation as bitterly as did the Vietnam War, fought in the 1960s and early 1970s. During that time, pro- and antiwar Americans argued and clashed on college campuses and on city streets. Antiwar protesters raged against the actions of the U.S. government, which was sending thousands of American troops to fight the communist forces of North Vietnam. Meanwhile, the American men and women in Vietnam attempted to do their duties, even if they did not understand the confusing politics behind the struggle.

In an emotional 1984 ceremony, Vietnam War veterans salute the remains of the Vietnam War's Unknown Soldier.

One dedicated Vietnam serviceman was air force officer Daniel "Chappie" James, Jr., who died in 1978 and was buried at Arlington. An African American, James joined the army air force in 1943, when the armed forces were still segregated. Overcoming prejudice, he became an officer and a splendid pilot. In Vietnam, he flew seventy-eight combat missions. After the war, James was promoted to four-star general, the first African American to achieve that rank.

In a 1972 ceremony, Daniel "Chappie" James is pinned with stars by his son (left) and wife (right). He became a four-star general, making him the first African American to achieve that rank in the history of the U.S. Air Force.

Left: Widow of a fallen Persian Gulf War soldier is presented with a folded American flag.

Below: This statue is an Arlington memorial to nurses who have served in the U.S. armed forces.

In the late 1990s, tensions between the United States and the Iraqi government reached a breaking point when Iraq invaded Kuwait, an ally of the United States. President George Bush ordered more than a half-million American troops to the Persian Gulf to repel the invading Iraqi forces. Partaking in the fury of this desert war was helicopter pilot Maria Rossi of New Jersey. Even though she knew she would have to fly in treacherous weather, Rossi volunteered for a difficult mission in March 1991. Early into the flight, her Chinook helicopter crashed, killing her and the crew she commanded. Inscribed on her headstone at Arlington is the message: "First Female Combat Commander to Fly in Battle." On the reverse side a plaque says, "May our men and women stand strong and equal."

The Apollo I *(left) and* Challenger *(right) crews*

The American effort to conquer outer space was not a war, but the crews manning space capsules faced the same perils as did combat soldiers. In 1967, all three men aboard *Apollo I* were killed when a fire swept through their craft while it was still on the ground. Two *Apollo I* crew members—Virgil Grissom and Roger Chaffee—were buried at Arlington, while the third—Edward White—was laid to rest at West Point. The men of *Apollo I* were part of a brave team of astronauts. Three of their crewmates eventually reached the moon in 1969.

Another tragedy struck the space program in January 1986, when the spacecraft *Challenger* exploded seventy-two seconds into its flight. All seven people aboard were killed, including Christa McAuliffe, a grade-school teacher who was to give classes via satellite television while in space. McAuliffe had described her space shuttle mission as "the ultimate field trip." A monument honoring the *Challenger* crew now stands at Arlington.

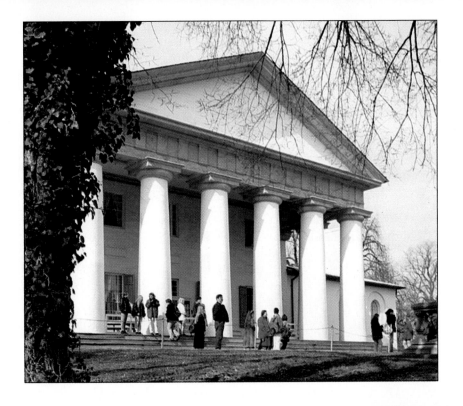

Built in 1817, Arlington House (left) stands on a high hill in Arlington National Cemetery. The house overlooks the Lincoln Memorial, the Reflecting Pool, and the Washington Monument in Washington, D.C.

Standing on a high hill in the center of Arlington National Cemetery is Arlington House. Many of its rooms have been stocked with period furniture to make them look as they did in 1861, when Robert E. Lee went to war. The front entrance to Arlington House presents a magnificent view of several Washington, D.C., landmarks. The city was planned and laid out in the late 1790s by Pierre Charles L'Enfant, a French architect hired by George Washington. In a remarkably forward-looking boast, L'Enfant told Washington he intended to design a capital so splendid it would serve "not for thirteen states, but for fifty." L'Enfant's grave stands in front of Arlington House, from which there is a grand vista of the city he helped to create.

Pierre Charles L'Enfant's grave

Schoolchildren visit the Eternal Flame that honors John F. Kennedy.

John F. Kennedy

Below Arlington House burns the Eternal Flame, which marks the grave of John F. Kennedy, the thirty-fifth president of the United States. Kennedy took office in 1961. He was young, vigorous, handsome, and he had the extraordinary ability to reach out to people and fill them with hope. As president, he once visited Arlington and found it so peaceful he said, "I could stay here forever." On November 22, 1963, Kennedy was struck down by an assassin's bullet in Dallas, Texas. After the cruel murder, a sense of shock paralyzed the country. Today, all Americans who lived through that time can recall exactly where they were and what they were doing when the terrible, unbelievable news came from Dallas.

In his 1961 inaugural address, Kennedy promised that his presidency "...will light our country and all who serve it, and the glow from that fire can truly light the world."

It is no wonder his grave is symbolized by the Eternal Flame.

Robert Kennedy

Near John F. Kennedy lies his brother, Robert Kennedy, whose grave is marked by a simple white cross. Robert had picked up John's banner and was running for president in the 1968 campaign. On June 6, Robert Kennedy was also murdered by an assassin. At the Arlington funeral, his brother, Edward, said, "Some men see things as they are and ask, 'Why?' He saw things that never were and asked, 'Why not?'"

The newest grave at the Kennedy plot belongs to Jacqueline Kennedy Onassis (the widow of John F. Kennedy), who died in 1994. Americans will never forget the dignity she displayed during her husband's funeral. Dressed in black, with her children at her side, she marched in the procession showing a quiet courage which gave people strength during a period of confusion and fear. Jacqueline Kennedy's memory rings proudly at Arlington, shrine of heroes.

John F. Kennedy, Jr. (kneeling), at the 1994 funeral of his mother, Jacqueline Kennedy Onassis

OTHER FAMOUS AMERICANS BURIED AT ARLINGTON NATIONAL CEMETERY

Omar Bradley
(1893–1981)
Popular World War II general who commanded Allied forces in Europe—the largest army ever assembled under the American flag

William Jennings Bryan
(1860–1925)
Famous orator, congressman, and leader of the Democratic Party from the 1890s through World War I; argued against lawyer Clarence Darrow in the famous Scopes "monkey trial" of 1925

Matthew Henson
(1867–1955)
African-American explorer who was the only American to accompany Robert Peary on the first successful expedition to the North Pole

George Marshall
(1880–1959)
American military general who was chief of staff for all American armed forces in World War II; later, as secretary of state, devised the "Marshall Plan," a program of American aid to help European economies recover after the war

Robert E. Peary
(1856–1920)
Former sailor in the U.S. Navy who later led a 1909 expedition that was the first to reach the North Pole

Walter Reed
(1851–1902)
Medical officer in the Spanish-American War who performed important experiments to discover the causes and cures of typhoid fever and yellow fever

Hyman G. Rickover
(1900–1986)
Naval officer who worked on designing the U.S.S. *Nautilus*, the first nuclear-powered submarine

William Howard Taft
(1857–1930)
Twenty-seventh president of the United States (1909–1913); the only president other than John F. Kennedy buried at Arlington

Earl Warren
(1891–1974)
Chief justice of the Supreme Court from 1953 to 1969; wrote the Court's 1954 opinion that outlawed racial segregation in public schools; also chaired the 1964 committee that produced the Warren Report, an investigation into President Kennedy's assassination.

A sentry is kept on duty at the Tomb of the Unknowns at all times.

One of the most moving experiences offered at Arlington is a visit to the Tomb of the Unknowns. Practically every war produces "unknowns"—soldiers whose bodies are so disfigured by bullets, bombs, or fire that they cannot be identified. In 1921, the remains of one such soldier, killed in World War I, were taken from a graveyard in France and re-buried at Arlington under a gleaming white sarcophagus bearing the words: HERE RESTS IN HONORED GLORY AN AMERICAN SOLDIER KNOWN BUT TO GOD.

The Unknown Soldier, being no one, could be anyone. Therefore, all the families who had lost a loved one whose remains could not be identified could worship at the grave of this unknown who represented all unknowns. In 1958, unknowns from World War II and Korea were buried at the site. An unknown from the Vietnam War was interred there in 1984.

Playing "Taps" at an Arlington funeral

The Tomb of the Unknowns is guarded by members of the Third Army Infantry, called "The Old Guard." During the day, an Old Guard sentinel marches twenty-one steps in front of the tomb, then stops and stares at the grave site for twenty-one seconds. This solemn ritual, watched by hundreds of silent tourists, is the equivalent of a twenty-one-gun military salute.

Flags almost always fly at half-mast at Arlington National Cemetery. In the distance, it is common to hear the lonesome refrain of a bugle sounding "Taps." About fifteen funerals are conducted on the grounds each day. Until the mid-1960s, anyone who had served honorably in the American armed forces and his or her spouse could be buried at Arlington. But available grave sites in the 612-acre cemetery grounds became scarce, and now burials require special approval.

Applicants who won medals in war or who were career members of the armed forces are given special consideration.

Across the Potomac River from the cemetery spreads the bustling, noisy city of Washington, D.C. Arlington, by contrast, is an island of tranquillity. Although the grounds are crowded with tourists during visiting hours, most guests are quiet, respectful of the dead. Private automobiles are not allowed in the cemetery. People walking amid the long rows of headstones tend to think silent thoughts of heroes, history, and the wastefulness of war. Many tourists ponder lines of poetry. One poem, written by a little-known poet named Theodore O'Hara, is an Arlington favorite. Its words are etched on plaques throughout the grounds:

> *On fame's eternal camping ground*
> *Their silent tents are spread*
> *And glory guards with solemn round*
> *The bivouac of the dead.*

TIMELINE

1775

Revolutionary War { **1778** .... Land for Arlington purchased
by John Parke Custis

1783

Arlington House completed **1817**

1861

American Civil War { **1864** ....

1865

Gen. Meigs selects
Arlington as national
cemetery site

Spanish-American War **1898**

1914
} World War I
1918

First "Unknown Soldier" buried at Arlington **1921**

1939
} World War II
Dec. 7: Japanese attack Pearl Harbor **1941**

1945

Korean War { **1950**

1953

John F. Kennedy assassinated **1963**   Vietnam War (heavy U.S. involvement:
mid-1960s–1973)
Apollo I explosion **1967**
Robert Kennedy assassinated **1968**

1975

1986

1991 Persian Gulf War

Challenger space
shuttle explosion

★ ★ ★ ★

CHAPTER 2

THE CAPITOL

ANDREW SANTELLA

The Capitol in Washington, D.C., is one of the most recognizable buildings in the world. Its splendid dome stands as a symbol of American democracy and self-government. The Capitol is where our elected representatives gather to make the laws by which we live. The great American writer Nathaniel Hawthorne once called the Capitol "the center and heart of America."

Construction on the Capitol began in 1793, when the United States was still a new nation. Over the next two hundred years, it was expanded, redesigned, and improved. After it was damaged by a fire, the Capitol was even rebuilt. Through the difficult years of the Civil War, construction continued on the Capitol's new dome. It served as a sign to Americans that the nation would endure.

Like American democracy itself, the Capitol building has been a work in progress. As the nation has changed and grown, the Capitol has grown with it. Today, the Capitol is more than 751 feet long and 350 feet wide. Its floor space covers over sixteen acres. At its highest point (the top of the statue *Freedom*), the Capitol is 287 feet tall. Inside, there are 850 doorways and 540 rooms, including chambers for the U.S. Senate and the U.S. House of Representatives.

The Capitol has been the site of some of the most important events in American history. After their deaths, many presidents have lain in state in the Capitol's great Rotunda. Nearly all the U.S. presidents since Andrew Jackson (in 1829) have been inaugurated on the Capitol steps. In 1835, an assassin attempted, but failed, to murder President Jackson as he was leaving the Capitol. In 1844, Samuel Morse first demonstrated his revolutionary invention, the telegraph, from the Capitol. He sent a message to his assistant, who was fifty miles away in Baltimore.

The body of President Dwight D. Eisenhower lies in state in the Capitol Rotunda in 1969.

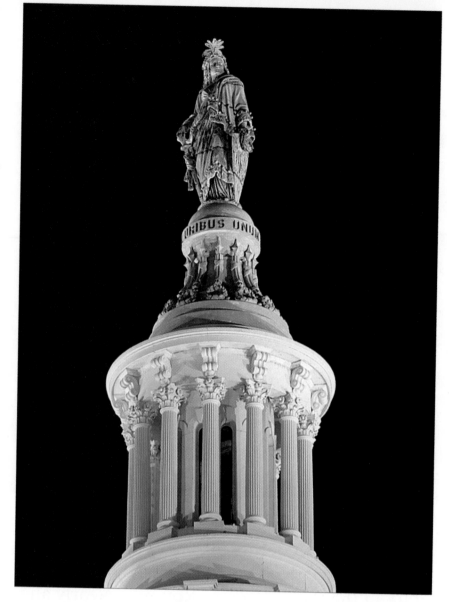

The statue Freedom *stands atop the Capitol dome. Inscribed at the base of the statue are the words* E Pluribus Unum.

At the base of the statue *Freedom* are inscribed the Latin words *E Pluribus Unum.* This means "Out of many, one." These words capture the spirit of the Capitol. It is here that representatives of all Americans meet to conduct the business of government. The work done by members of Congress ensures that the many different voices of the United States will be heard and will help shape a unified nation.

The story of the Capitol begins with the U.S. Constitution. In 1787, the writers of the Constitution allowed for a permanent home for the federal government, but they did not specify where this home would be established. After much debate, Congress finally passed the Residence Act in 1790. This law stated that the government would take residence on the banks of the Potomac River, between Virginia and Maryland. At the time, the nation's capital was New York City. The new capital city would be named Washington, in honor of the nation's first president and hero of the Revolutionary War.

This map, drawn in the 1790s, shows how architect Pierre Charles L'Enfant envisioned the street grid of the capital city. Just as L'Enfant designed it, the Capitol and the White House (called the President's House on this map) are both positioned along Pennsylvania Avenue in today's Washington, D.C.

Pierre Charles L'Enfant

Even though the Capitol is a historic American building, its first designer was a French engineer. The commissioners in charge of constructing new government buildings in Washington hired the talented French engineer Pierre Charles L'Enfant. They asked him to develop a plan for the new city, to design the important government buildings, and to oversee their construction.

L'Enfant produced an ambitious plan for Washington, D.C. It included grand plazas, public squares, and parks connected by wide boulevards. For the Capitol building, L'Enfant selected a site known as Jenkins Hill. He called it "a pedestal waiting for a monument." On a June morning in 1791, L'Enfant and President George Washington rode there on horseback. The president was impressed, and he urged L'Enfant to go forward with his plan. The stubborn L'Enfant, however, refused to produce an actual plan for the building, claiming he carried his ideas "in his head." L'Enfant had several other disagreements with the commissioners, and they

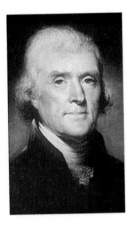

Thomas Jefferson

fired him in 1792.

The government now had to look for another architect to design its home. Secretary of State Thomas Jefferson, himself an amateur architect, suggested that the government hold a design competition. The architect with the best design would win the prize of $500 and a city lot. The competition drew at least sixteen entries. Some of the designs were quite imaginative. One showed a giant rooster weathervane crowing from the roof of the building. Although some of the designs were impressive, none were quite right for the future home of the United States government.

Several months after the competition deadline, a doctor from the British West Indies named William Thornton was allowed to submit his design. Although he made his living as a doctor, Thornton had a talent for painting and architecture. His design "captivated the eyes and judgment of all," said Jefferson. President Washington praised it for its "grandeur, simplicity, and convenience."

Opposite Page: One of the Capitol designs not chosen Below: William Thornton's winning design

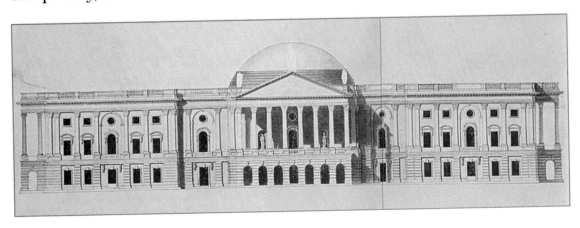

Thornton's design called for a domed central building that was modeled on the Pantheon, a famous temple of ancient Rome. Thornton designed two wings on each side of the building—one to house the Senate, and one for the House of Representatives.

Workmen began digging foundations for the Capitol in August 1793. On September 18, 1793, President Washington laid the cornerstone of the building and construction began. Work proceeded so slowly, however, that construction was continually behind schedule. To be lured from their homes to the new city of Washington, workers had to be paid higher wages than usual.

George Washington lays the cornerstone for the Capitol, a ceremony that marks the beginning of a building's construction.

The heavy sandstone used for some parts of the building had to be brought to the site by boat. Some boats were so overloaded that they sank on the way to the construction site. And the builders were continually running short of money to fund the project.

Because of these and other problems, the commissioners had to halt construction and change their plans. In 1796, they decided to abandon work on the domed center building and South Wing that Thornton had planned. Instead, they concentrated on completing the North Wing. With Congress scheduled to move into the Capitol in 1800, they reasoned that it would be better to have one completed wing than to have all three unfinished.

Even though William Thornton's design was very popular, the commissioners decided that a more experienced architect was needed to oversee the construction. They hired two architects, but both were immediately fired because they asked for too many changes to the design. Finally, a third architect, James Hoban, was brought in to complete this initial stage of building. (Hoban had designed the President's House, later called the White House, in 1792.)

By 1800, the North Wing of the Capitol was complete, except for some of the rooms on the third floor. The Senate, the House of Representatives, the Supreme Court, the Library of Congress, and the district courts all squeezed into their cramped new home. Congress convened there for the first time on November 21, 1800. The next day, President John Adams addressed Congress. He said he wanted to officially "congratulate the people of the United States on the assembling of Congress at their permanent seat of government."

For the 106 representatives and 32 senators gathered there, the building quickly became overcrowded. To ease the situation, they tried a number of temporary solutions. For instance, the House of Representatives met for several years in a different building. It was so stuffy and overheated that it was nicknamed "the Oven."

Fortunately, construction on the other permanent wings of the Capitol was continuing. In 1803, President Thomas Jefferson appointed Benjamin Latrobe architect of the Capitol. The same year, Congress set aside $50,000 to help speed construction of its new home. In 1807, Latrobe finally completed the South Wing, which included his magnificent Hall of the House, where the House of Representatives would meet. President Jefferson and others praised Latrobe's work, but some critics were not impressed. Representative John Randolph of Virginia complained that echoes in the Hall of the House made it almost impossible to hear speakers.

Benjamin Henry Latrobe was the second person appointed to the position of architect of the Capitol; the first was William Thornton. In the country's early years, the architect of the Capitol was responsible for overseeing the construction and expansion of the Capitol building, itself. In later years, the men who held this position also designed the buildings that house the Library of Congress, the Supreme Court, and the U.S. Botanic Garden, among many others.

Congress soon faced a crisis that would change the history of the young republic and its Capitol. The United States and Great Britain were engaged in a dispute because the British were unlawfully detaining American sailors. On June 18, 1812, Congress declared war on Great Britain. The conflict came to be known as the War of 1812.

The British invasion left the Capitol heavily damaged, but still standing.

For two years, the war was fought far from Washington. But in the summer of 1814, a British force landed in Maryland and marched to Washington. Not only did they capture the city, they burned most of it to the ground. The Capitol did not escape damage. Most of its interior was destroyed. However, a sudden rainstorm prevented the building from being completely burned down.

The British soon left the city, and by that fall Congress was again meeting in Washington— this time in a former hotel. For the next four years, Congress met in a quickly constructed building called the "Brick Capitol."

★ ★ ★ ★

When Benjamin Latrobe came back to Washington and saw the damaged Capitol, he called it "a most magnificent ruin." He then set to work restoring the ruin.

Smoke-darkened stones were scrubbed clean. Those that were beyond rescue were replaced. The House Chamber was redesigned, and the Senate Chamber was enlarged and beautified. Latrobe could not make all the changes he wanted, however. When the commissioner of public buildings would not approve some of his plans for the Senate and House Chambers, Latrobe resigned in 1817.

The "Brick Capitol," the building where Congress met while the Capitol was repaired

Charles Bulfinch

The next year, Charles Bulfinch was hired to replace Latrobe as architect of the Capitol. Bulfinch immediately began working on the long-awaited center building that would finally connect the North and South wings. Both Thornton and Latrobe had left behind designs for the center building, but Bulfinch had his own ideas. His Rotunda, a large circular hall, was topped by a wooden dome covered in copper. In 1824, the Rotunda was opened. By 1826, after thirty-seven years of construction, the Capitol was complete.

An 1830s view of the Capitol's magnificent Rotunda

For the next twenty years, no major work was done on the Capitol. But the nation itself grew at an amazing rate. New states entered the Union, and the country's population nearly doubled between 1840 and 1860. As the population grew, so did the number of congressmen. By 1850, 62 senators and 232 representatives sat in Congress. The chambers they occupied were not designed to accommodate such large numbers. So Congress approved an expansion of the original wings of the Capitol.

The earliest known photograph of the Capitol, taken in 1846, shows the Rotunda topped with its old, wooden dome.

President Millard Fillmore appointed Thomas U. Walter architect of the Capitol in 1851. Walter's expansion doubled the size of the building by adding to the wings on either side of the center building. He designed new chambers for both the Senate and the House of Representatives. He beautified the interior of the Capitol. But the most visible change of all was the larger, cast-iron dome he designed to replace the old, wooden one.

The House moved into its new home in 1857 and the Senate took up its new residence in 1859. But even as these plans for the future moved forward, the nation was facing the worst crisis it ever encountered. The conflict between the southern and northern states threatened the very existence of the Union. In 1861, the Civil War began, pitting the South against the North.

At the beginning of the war, the Capitol was turned into a makeshift barracks for Union (northern) troops. They called their headquarters the "Big Tent." As many as 3,000 soldiers were quartered in the building at one time. Basement meeting rooms were turned into a bakery to supply bread for the troops. The Capitol was also used as an emergency hospital for the wounded.

As the war raged on, construction on the Capitol's new dome continued. President Abraham Lincoln was initially criticized for spending money on the dome while the nation

Construction equipment was visible at President Abraham Lincoln's first inauguration in 1861 (top). The wooden Capitol dome was being replaced with an iron dome (bottom).

was involved in a brutal war. But Lincoln defended himself, claiming that the Capitol dome was a symbol of national unity. "If the people see the Capitol [construction] going on," Lincoln said, "they will take it as a sign that the Union will go on." The same dome that was constructed during the Civil War tops the Capitol today. The dome is actually made of two fitted cast-iron shells. Together, they weigh nearly nine million pounds.

When the dome was finished in 1863, it was topped by the statue *Freedom*, the work of American artist Thomas Crawford. The enormous bronze figure is over nineteen feet tall. It stood throughout the last years of the Civil War and remains atop the Capitol today, fulfilling President Lincoln's vision.

Above: Thomas Crawford
Right: A design sketch for Crawford's statue Freedom

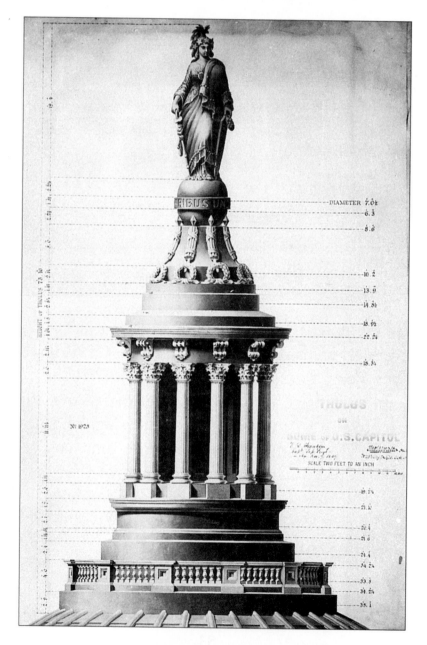

* * * *

Since the Civil War, many modern facilities have been installed in the Capitol. Indoor plumbing was added in 1865, and by 1900 the Capitol had electricity in every room. Air conditioning was installed in 1929. Since the iron dome was added in 1863, however, there have been few major renovations to the exterior. In 1959, a new marble front was added to the east side of the building, about thirty-two feet east of the original sandstone wall. The alteration provided more space and gave the building a more balanced appearance.

Over the years, the federal government has outgrown the walls of the Capitol, which is in the center of this photograph. The two buildings to the left house the Library of Congress. The buildings to the right house the offices of the U.S. Senate. Offices for members of the House of Representatives are located in other buildings near the Capitol.

In 1976, a major restoration project was completed on the Capitol. As part of the country's 200th birthday celebration, the old House, Senate, and Supreme Court chambers were returned to their original condition. And from 1983 to 1987, the western exterior walls were cleaned, weatherproofed, and restored.

In the 1980s, the west front of the Capitol was restored and covered by marble. This was done because the old sandstone walls had deteriorated over the years.

*Top: Senators ride a
private subway
to the Capitol from
a Senate office
building in 1922.*

*Bottom: New
subway trains were
installed in 1994 to
connect the Capitol
to several nearby
office buildings.*

Today, the Capitol operates in a way that
would amaze the building's original designers of
two centuries ago. The Capitol is almost a self-
contained city, housing everything from a post
office to barber shops and banks. The building
even has its own power plant. Congress's 100
senators and 435 representatives travel to
and from their office buildings on a private
subway. They are protected by a special Capitol
police force.

The magnificent view looking up from the floor of the Rotunda

Modern technology allows every U.S. citizen to "visit" the Capitol every day. Broadcasts of House and Senate sessions are carried on cable television in virtually every American community. And in 1995, the Library of Congress made available on the Internet the full text of all congressional acts and debates.

* * * *

The Capitol building is open to visitors from across the nation and around the world. People walk through the magnificent Rotunda, which is home to many historic paintings and statues. Looking up, visitors see the interior of Thomas Walter's tremendous dome. The ceiling of the dome is covered with artist Constantino Brumidi's magnificent painting called *The Apotheosis of George Washington.* The painting covers 4,664 square feet, and depicts Greek gods and goddesses with famous figures from American history. For

Italian-born artist Constantino Brumidi's spectacular painting The Apotheosis of George Washington, *which caps the interior of the dome*

twenty-five years, Brumidi created numerous paintings and sculptures that still decorate the walls, ceilings, and corridors of the Capitol. Priceless works of many other artists make their home at the Capitol.

Right: The walls and ceiling of this hallway are decorated with paintings of Constantino Brumidi. Below: Randolph Rogers's famous Columbus Doors, upon which each bronze panel features a different event in Christopher Columbus's life. Bottom: a closeup of the doors' bottom left panel, depicting Columbus on trial.

Left: Visitors in the National Statuary Hall

Bottom: The statues of (left to right) Alexander Stephens (representing Georgia), Brigham Young (Utah), Ethan Allen (Vermont), George Shoup (Idaho), and John C. Calhoun (South Carolina)

The National Statuary Hall is another popular attraction on visitors' tours of the Capitol. This hall was originally Benjamin Latrobe's Hall of the House. In 1864, it became a room to showcase bronze and marble statues honoring distinguished citizens from every state in the nation. Standing in the hall today are statues of such heroes as Utah's religious leader Brigham Young and Vermont's Revolutionary War hero Ethan Allen.

New members of Congress are sworn into office.

From its very beginnings, the Capitol has been a treasured national symbol. It is also where the daily work of the United States government is done. It is where our democratic ideals become reality. The Capitol is such an enduring symbol that many people and organizations ask to purchase the American flags that fly over the Capitol. To accommodate all the requests, employees of the Capitol's architect's office raise and lower thousands of flags each year for shipment. In one year, more than 97,000 flags were raised and lowered. That's about 268 flags a day! These flags are special simply because they have flown briefly over one of the most important buildings in U.S. history—the Capitol. Thomas Jefferson was correct two hundred years ago, when he predicted that the Capitol would captivate all who saw it.

TIMELINE

Construction begins on the Capitol

1787	U.S. Constitution signed
1790	Residence Act passed by Congress
1793	
1800	North Wing completed; Congress convenes
1803	Benjamin Latrobe appointed architect
1807	South Wing completed

War of 1812 {
1812	
1814	Capitol nearly destroyed by British troops

1824	Wooden dome completed

Construction of Capitol completed **1826**

1857	House of Representatives extension built

Senate extension built **1859**

New dome completed **1863**

} American Civil War

1861	
1865	

Elevators installed in Capitol **1874**

Supreme Court moves out of Capitol and into new building **1935**

East Front of Capitol extended **1959**

1976

Capitol exterior restored **1987**

Old House, Senate, and Supreme Court chambers restored

★ ★ ★ ★

Chapter 3

Ellis Island

Judith Jango-Cohen

It is 1907. A small girl stands at the railing of a ship, gripping a ball of yarn in her hands. On shore, another girl holds the end of the yarn. As the ship slips away, the ball of yarn unwinds. The girls do not hear the passengers' good-bye cries. They do not see the waving handkerchiefs or the babies lifted high. Each watches her friend shrinking smaller and smaller. Soon the last bit of yarn flies from the traveler's hands. It flutters above the ship, waving on the wind. The girl's tears dry in the salty air as her home in Italy disappears.

Nine days later the ship enters New York Harbor in the United States of America. America is where many passengers hope to make a new home. Most will pass through Ellis Island. On the island, they will receive permission to stay in America or they will be turned away.

The **immigrants** carry battered baskets and bulging sacks, holding precious pieces of their past. A young woman has packed a photograph and a strand of hair from her baby who has died. Others bring symbols of their faith, such as a golden cross or a silver menorah. People have packed favorite books, tin soldiers, dolls, and musical instruments. They take hand-stitched clothes and down quilts.

From 1892 to 1954, Ellis Island served as the gateway to the United States for millions of immigrants.

A Polish immigrant carries a single trunk with his most prized possessions.

There are also those with no belongings. One Jewish family, fleeing from Russia, has borrowed an empty suitcase. They do not want others to know that they have nothing. But even those with no possessions carry three things with them. Each person brings courage, hope, and a story.

In 1915, a group of Armenian children board a ship. They are leaving to seek safety in other countries.

A Russian girl hides in her basement, struggling to quiet her baby sister. Soldiers have come to rob the house and kill her family because they are Jewish. Cleverly, her father has set out bottles of whiskey to distract the soldiers. While the soldiers drink, the family slips away. During the night, they hurry to the train station. The train takes them to a seaport where they board a ship to America.

In the late 1800s and early 1900s, millions of immigrants left their homelands in Europe and journeyed to America. Some, such as Russian Jews, fled from religious or racial **persecution**. The Armenians in Turkey were another such group. In March 1915, the Muslim Turkish government announced a decision to rid Turkey of all the Christian Armenians. Some Armenians were murdered in their homes. Others were marched into the desert, where they died of hunger or thirst. Between 1915 and

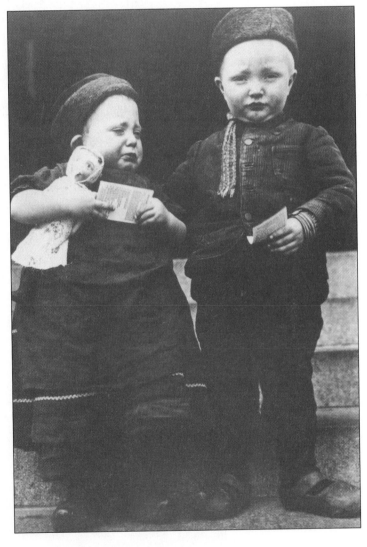

These two Dutch children arrived on Ellis Island in 1906.

1923 the Turkish government killed more than one million Armenians.

Hunger drove other immigrants across the sea to America. Europe's population was growing, and there were not enough jobs for everyone. People in cities found it difficult to feed their families. In the countryside, wealthy people owned much of the farmland. People who worked for them earned barely enough money to survive.

Some immigrants came because harsh rulers gave them little freedom in their own countries. Benito Mussolini, for example, controlled the government in Italy. He also controlled the newspapers, radio programs, and movies, allowing no one to speak out against him.

Benito Mussolini came to power in Italy in 1922. Some Italians left their country to escape his harsh rule.

The United States became a refuge for people from many countries. In America, immigrants bought land and started their own farms. In growing cities, they found jobs building roads, bridges, and parks. They voted for the leaders of their choice. They were free to say what they believed, and they worshipped as they pleased. Escaping death and despair, they found freedom from want and freedom from fear.

Millions of immigrants left their homes, friends, and sometimes families in hopes of building a better life in the United States.

GOD BLESS AMERICA

Many immigrants felt that coming to America was like opening a door to a new life. For immigrants who could not speak English and had no education, that life was difficult. But hardships did not break them. In fact, many immigrants became famous. Songwriter Irving Berlin was a Russian Jew who came to the United States in 1893. He would later write one of our country's most beloved songs, "God Bless America."

* * * *

Immigrants sailed into seaports throughout America. They arrived in cities such as Boston, Baltimore, Philadelphia, New Orleans, Seattle, and San Francisco. The nation's biggest and busiest port was New York.

Swamped with immigrants, New York was the first of these ports to open a receiving station. In 1855, the state set up Castle Garden on the southern tip of Manhattan. At Castle Garden, immigrants could exchange their own money for American dollars. They could also buy railroad tickets to other cities. If they were staying in the city, they could obtain information about jobs and housing there.

A group of immigrants arrives in New York Harbor in 1878.

Castle Garden, shown here in 1851, served as the entry point for immigrants from 1855 to 1890. It previously served as an Army fort and an opera house.

Between 1880 and 1900 about nine million immigrants entered the United States. These record-breaking waves of immigrants made some Americans uneasy. They wanted laws passed to control the number of people who could enter the country.

In 1891, the United States government created the Bureau of Immigration. This organization would take charge of the immigration process. The government also passed a law rejecting certain immigrants, including criminals, people with a serious **contagious** disease, and those who could not support themselves due to mental or physical illness.

New York was receiving about 75 percent of America's immigrants. As a result, it needed a bigger immigration station. Some people felt that the harbor islands would be an ideal location. There, people could be kept off the mainland

This photograph shows Ellis Island in 1897, before the fire.

while being inspected for admission to America. Bedloe's Island, now called Liberty Island, was suggested, but it was already home to the Statue of Liberty. Instead, the honor fell to its neighbor Ellis Island, about 1 mile (1.6 kilometers) west of Castle Garden.

Construction of the Ellis Island Immigration Station began in 1890. In January 1892, the immigration station was completed. Twelve new buildings stood on the island, including the main receiving building, four hospital buildings, a restaurant, and a kitchen.

The station did not serve immigrants for long. One June evening in 1897, people looking across the water at Ellis

Island saw a startling sight. The *New York Sun* reported, "Flames were shooting a hundred feet in the air, and by their light hundreds of people could be seen on the island running hither and thither." Luckily, the inspection station was not busy. Ferries rescued the staff and all 140 immigrants. But the wooden station was a charred ruin.

One month after the fire, construction began on a new immigration station. The Barge Office, near Castle Garden, served as a receiving station during this time. The new brick and stone building, still standing today, opened on December 17, 1900.

The Barge Office was used as a temporary immigration station from 1897 to 1900.

THE EARLY YEARS

Ellis Island was a busy place even before it became home to the immigration station. Samuel Ellis, a businessman, owned the land during the American Revolution. In 1810, the United States government bought the island and built a fort. The fort guarded New York Harbor during the War of 1812. After the war Ellis Island was used as a place to store **explosives**. Nearby residents of New Jersey and New York were relieved to see the explosives removed for the construction of the immigration station.

When the new immigration station opened in 1900, airplanes did not yet exist. Immigrants had to travel across the sea in ships. Before the 1920s most ships sold three types of tickets: first-class, second-class, and steerage.

First-class tickets were the most expensive. Wealthy passengers stayed in roomy cabins with running water. They ate in dining rooms and were served fancy meals that were cooked by skilled chefs. Second-class passengers stayed in similar cabins that were slightly less grand.

In 1920, more than two thousand Italian immigrants crowd the deck of the S.S. Regina de Italia for their first glimpse of the U.S.

The least expensive way to travel on most ships was in **steerage**. The steerage area was in the dark "basement" of the boat near the steering equipment. Before the 1920s

there were no cabins in steerage. It was simply an open area lined with rows of bunks. By 1922, ships had built third-class cabins in their lowest levels.

Most immigrants could afford only steerage. Some shipping companies stuffed in two or three times as many people as could reasonably fit. Passengers slept on mattresses made from bags of straw or seaweed. Life preservers became pillows. Often, toilets were just a pit. Steerage was usually never cleaned, even though people ate and slept there. The smell was so thick and strong, people felt as if they could touch it.

Conditions aboard the steamships were not ideal. Tired men, women, and children endured dirty, overcrowded conditions for weeks at a time.

Some shipping companies let passengers set sail on leaky boats. Many people, especially children, got sick on these waterlogged ships. Because of the wet, filthy conditions, they sometimes died. With horror, immigrants watched as the crew threw the small bodies of children into the water.

Other more fortunate people had happy memories of their voyage. Children swung on rope swings that sailors set up for them.

Children play onboard the Friedrich der Grosse, a German ship.

Some played with pets that they had sneaked onboard. Others gathered together to sing and recite poems. Even people speaking different languages managed to feel close. One man said that when people patted him on the head or gave him a hug, he knew they were friends.

Most immigrants met stormy weather on their voyage. Choppy waves made many people seasick. But bad weather could do something much worse—it could sink a ship. As heaving seas tossed the boat up and down, passengers prayed and cast religious medals into the water. One woman and her brother remember being told that their ship was likely to go down. But the misery they had been through in their own country had taught them to have courage. So when the sailor gave them the terrifying news, the two responded, "We will dance."

Somehow, their storm-battered ship stayed afloat. When it later sailed into New York Harbor, people streamed toward the railing to see the Statue of Liberty. "Please, everybody, we should move a little bit to the center!" the captain pleaded. He feared that the unbalanced ship would surely sink. But everyone was crying, and nobody moved. Jews stood in their prayer shawls, and Christians knelt,

The Statue of Liberty was many immigrants' first welcome to the U.S.

STOWAWAYS

Most ships had **stowaways** hiding onboard. The most determined stowaway held at Ellis Island was fourteen-year-old Michael Gilhooley. Gilhooley was a Belgian boy whose mother had died during World War I. In 1919, Gilhooley stowed away five times, hoping to start a new life in America. Each time he was discovered and returned to Belgium. American newspapers printed his story, and hundreds offered to help. Finally, officials placed him in the care of a wealthy New York woman. Soon the former stowaway was riding through the city in a fancy limousine.

Ship officials search for stowaways among the baggage.

making the sign of the cross. One woman remembers seeing the Statue of Liberty opening her arms to all the immigrants. The woman begged the beautiful lady to give her a chance to do something, to be somebody in America.

People sailing into New York may have felt that the Statue of Liberty was welcoming them to America, but they hadn't been accepted just yet. First, the inspectors of the Bureau

82

of Immigration had to decide if an immigrant was "clearly and without a doubt **entitled** to land."

When a ship anchored in the harbor, doctors and inspectors went out to meet it. Doctors separated all who were sick and sent them to hospitals on the island. Those with contagious diseases were sent into New York City until a contagious disease hospital opened at the station in 1911.

Immigrants with scarlet fever are removed from the S.S. Lapland and brought to the hospital at Ellis Island.

* * * *

Inspectors briefly questioned the first- and second-class passengers. Most were quickly cleared because the government saw little risk in admitting these wealthy people to the United States. When the boat docked, they were free to go. Steerage and third-class passengers had to endure a more lengthy inspection on Ellis Island.

Sometimes thousands of immigrants arrived at once. People had to wait aboard ship for hours or even days until a barge could take them to the island. Friends and family already living in America sometimes passed by in little boats. Immigrants lowered baskets to the boats and hauled up treats from their visitors.

Steerage passengers had to undergo lengthy questioning by Ellis Island officials.

Immigrants board a ferry that will take them to Ellis Island.

When the ship was allowed to dock, people boarded a barge to Ellis Island. If the inspection station were full, people waited on these barges. "We were jammed in so tight that I couldn't turn 'round," one immigrant recalled. Besides being crowded, barges lacked enough seats, drinking water, and toilets. They also provided no protection from summer sun or winter winds.

At last, people stepped onto Ellis Island. All had different impressions as they entered the castle-like building with copper-domed towers. One man described it as big enough to hold everyone in his village as well as their cattle. Many remembered the confusion of boxes, bundles, and endless rows of benches. There were babies screaming, children running, and nervous families huddled

THE GOLDEN DOOR

The Statue of Liberty has graced New York Harbor since 1886. A poem called "The New Colossus" is inscribed on the pedestal. It was written by Emma Lazarus, an author who was inspired by the courageous immigrants seeking freedom in America. Its most famous lines read:

Give me your tired,

your poor,

Your huddled masses

yearning to

breathe free,

The wretched refuse of

your teeming shore.

Send these, the homeless,

tempest-tost to me,

I lift my lamp beside the

golden door!

The Statue of Liberty was a gift from France to the United States. It serves as a symbol of the liberty both countries treasure.

together. Inspectors with blue coats and brass buttons dashed back and forth.

The uniformed watchmen and doctors scared many immigrants. Their uniforms reminded some people of the police and soldiers who had persecuted them back home. One man explained that in his country, a person in uniform was not someone who would help him. It was someone who might cut off his head.

Upon entering the immigration station, everyone lined up for a medical exam. Doctors watched immigrants for signs of limping, unsteadiness, and difficulty breathing. They inspected skin and scalp for infections. Doctors also questioned people

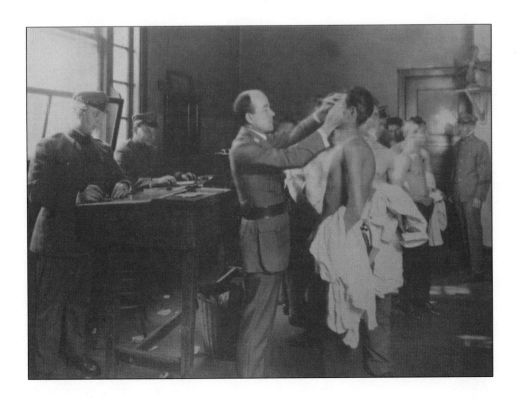

Doctors perform physical checkups on male immigrants at Ellis Island.

to check their hearing and speech. If immigrants did not speak English, **interpreters** helped out.

Other doctors examined people's eyes. They were on the alert for diseases like trachoma. This contagious infection could cause blindness if not treated. Using a little hook, or sometimes their fingers, doctors lifted a person's eyelids. Most immigrants feared this exam. They knew that if trachoma were discovered, they would be sent back to their homeland. They also dreaded the exam because it was painful.

A US Public Health doctor examines children upon arrival at Ellis Island.

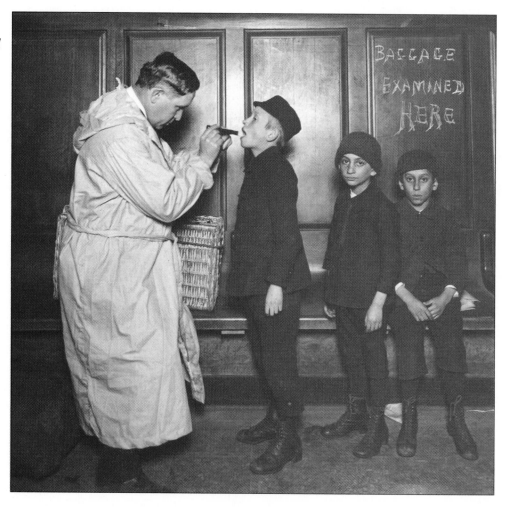

One immigrant performs a mental test in order to pass inspection. Puzzles were often used because an immigrant did not need to know how to read or write in order to do them.

One woman, who was five at the time, recalls being terrified. A man had jokingly told her that when they examined his eyes, one eyeball fell into his pocket.

When doctors suspected a problem, they marked the person's shoulder or back with chalk. Each medical condition was coded with letters. *CT* stood for trachoma, *Sc* for scalp infection, *H* for heart problems, and *X* for a suspected mental illness.

One woman remembers the fright of seeing a chalk mark on her sister's coat. "If they **deported** my sister," she thought, "where would she go?" Luckily, the little girl had a fancy coat with a silk lining. At the advice of a kind stranger, she turned her coat inside out. This saved her from being taken from the line for a closer inspection.

At Ellis Island, doctors had to determine if an immigrant was mentally as well as physically fit. To measure mental health and intelligence, they asked

BITING BUGS

Lice were a common medical problem at Ellis Island. These biting bugs easily spread from person to person in the tightly packed ships and crowded immigration station. Lice not only made people itchy, they also spread a disease called **typhus**. With immigrants continuously coming in, it was difficult to rid the station of these blood-sucking insects.

simple questions, such as "How much is two plus two?" One girl was asked if it were better to wash stairs from top to bottom or from bottom to top. The young girl did not understand that this was an intelligence question. She replied, "I don't go to America to wash stairs."

If doctors suspected mental illness or low intelligence, the people in question were asked to take special exams. Sometimes they had to put puzzles together. They also took memory tests. If immigrants failed the mental exams three times, they were rejected. Some inspectors felt that these exams were not always fair. There were immigrants who knew the answers but did not respond because they were frightened.

A legal inspection was another hurdle for immigrants. While awaiting their inspection, people crowded into the tremendous, flag-draped Registry Room. Each person was led to one of the bench-lined

This is a 1924 photo of the Registry Room at Ellis Island. The commotion and crowds in this "great hall" could make it a frightening place.

rows. Then they waited in the noisy hall for their names to be called. At the head of each row an inspector sat behind a large desk on a high stool. Each inspector had a list from the steamship companies with information about passengers. Inspectors asked immigrants for their name, place of birth, age, occupation (job), and destination. Most people were headed for places where friends or family lived.

Inspectors also asked questions that needed a yes or no answer. A yes answer to certain questions could lead to deportation. One question was, "Have you ever been in jail?"

They also asked people if they already had a job waiting for them in America. Beginning in 1885, it was illegal for American employers to bring over workers. American

New arrivals line up to have their papers examined by inspectors.

Shown here, immigrants anxiously wait in line to answer the inspector's questions.

workers did not want to lose their jobs to immigrants, who were willing to work for lower wages than Americans. Even low wages in America were higher than the wages most immigrants were earning in their homelands.

Some inspectors asked to see how much money an immigrant had. They wanted proof that immigrants had enough money to take care of themselves in America. To be safe, some people exchanged their second-class ticket for third-class before leaving. This

THIEVES

Bewildered immigrants on Ellis Island were easy prey for thieves. Crooks would come over from New York City disguised in official-looking caps and jackets. "May I help you with your suitcase?" they would ask a woman, who would never see her belongings again. "Let me see your money!" another would demand, taking an immigrant's fifty-dollar bill. "It's no good," the thief would say, giving him or her four bright pennies in return.

way they had extra money to show the inspector. For those who did not have the money, bills were sometimes passed from one person to another. "This had to be done with a quick motion of the hand so no one would get caught," a man remembered. Immigrants often helped each other in these trying moments.

Immigrants who did not pass the legal or medical inspections had to appear before a group of inspectors. These inspectors, who formed a board of special inquiry, made the final decision. Each board's three inspectors and an interpreter heard the cases of

Two immigrants face a board of special inquiry.

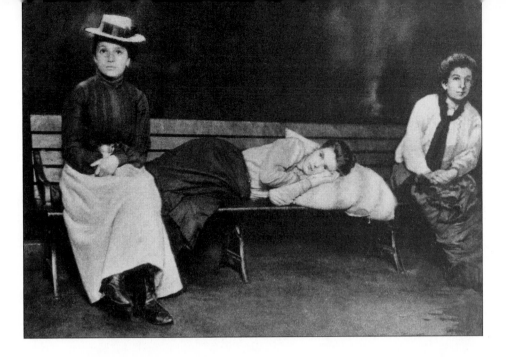

Sometimes immigrants were rejected by officials at Ellis Island. These three women are waiting for a steamship to take them back to their home country.

between fifty to one hundred immigrants each day.

One elderly woman, for example, could not figure out the puzzles. During the questioning, the woman convinced the board that she was worthy of admittance. She promised to show the inspectors that she could make them a delicious soup and could bake finer bread than they served on Ellis Island.

Not all cases turned out as well. One woman still remembers when the inspectors discovered that her grandmother had a black nail. "She raised us, all the years, with that hand and with that nail. There was nothing wrong with it. And they held her back . . . So we never saw her again . . . I'm still crying over it."

Only about 2 percent of the twelve million people who passed through Ellis Island were deported. But that amounted to about one quarter of a million people. Fiorello La Guardia, who later became mayor of New York City, was once an interpreter at Ellis Island. He wrote: "The immigration laws were rigidly enforced, and there

★ ★ ★ ★

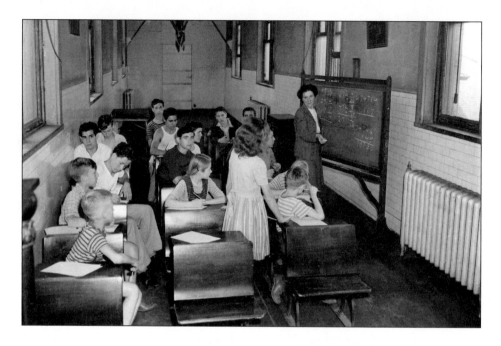

Some immigrants were held at Ellis Island for months. Here, a group of young detainees attend classes led by a social worker on the island.

AID FOR IMMIGRANTS

Groups called immigrant aid societies helped to ease the fear that gripped many immigrants. Members of aid societies explained problems when interpreters were unavailable. They assisted people in getting jobs and helped contact friends and relatives. They also did small favors, such as giving crackers, doughnuts, and milk to hungry children.

were many heartbreaking scenes on Ellis Island. I never managed . . . to become **callous** to the mental anguish, the disappointment, and the despair I witnessed almost daily."

The inspection process was often a whirlwind of fear and confusion. For many immigrants it only lasted a short while. Some immigrants, though, were **detained** on the island for days, weeks, or even months.

People were detained for several reasons. About half of those detained were awaiting a hearing before a board of special inquiry. Others were recovering from illness in the hospital. Some were waiting for train fare to arrive from family or friends already in the country. Women and children under sixteen could not leave until a relative came for them.

Feeding all the detained people was a huge job. On busy days, the Ellis Island staff served three meals a day to three thousand people. During its six decades of operation, the food service quality varied. Some immigrants endured meals of rye bread and prunes served in dirty dining halls. Others were more fortunate. One woman still remembers a fish dinner with bread, butter, and big pitchers of milk. Foods such as white bread, gelatin, ice cream, hot dogs, and bananas were strange to many immigrants. Some people mistakenly ate bananas without peeling them first!

This photograph, taken in the early 1900s, shows immigrants having lunch at Ellis Island.

Sleeping conditions varied over the years as well. At times, bedbugs and lice tormented weary immigrants. People squeezed into narrow metal bunks stacked three rows high. In later, less crowded times, **detainees** slept comfortably on single beds with spotless blankets and sheets.

Immigrants gradually left Ellis Island. Relatives or needed funds arrived. People got well. Boards announced their decisions. Every morning inspectors read the names of those who were to be admitted to America. One man still remembers the moment when they called his family's name. Everyone jumped up and down and cried. That was all they wanted to hear.

This photograph shows the sleeping quarters as it looked in 1923. In busier years sleeping areas were not as comfortable.

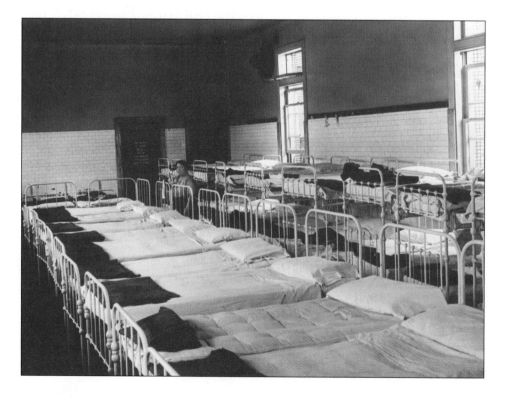

At times, Ellis Island had more people than it had space. This picture was taken in 1920, when the station was so crowded it had to be closed for a short time.

"HUMAN TIDE"

As the twentieth century rolled in, huge numbers of immigrants flocked to Ellis Island. Its busiest year was 1907, when about one million immigrants entered New York Harbor. On May 2, more than twenty-one thousand immigrants waited onboard ships. Dining halls, built to serve eight hundred, served three thousand at one meal. Inspectors said they felt swamped by a human tide, as they sometimes examined a stream of four to five hundred immigrants per day.

All Americans did not greet immigrants warmly in the 1900s. Some Americans were afraid of losing their jobs to immigrants, who would work for lower wages. Others disliked the "new" type of immigrant coming in. In the late 1800s most immigrants came from countries in northern and western Europe, including England, Ireland, Germany, Sweden, and Norway. During the twentieth century many came from

A Hungarian mother and her children posed for this photo upon their arrival at Ellis Island in 1909.

southern and eastern European countries such as Italy, Russia, Poland, Hungary, and Austria.

In 1894, a group of wealthy Americans founded the Immigration Restriction League. These people felt that the "new" immigrants were "polluting" the blood of America. In response to the alarm and anger of groups like this one, Congress passed the Immigration Act of 1917. Thereafter, all immigrants aged sixteen and older would have to pass a reading test to be admitted into the United States. The league hoped that this test would block many immigrants from entry.

Four years later, Congress passed the Quota Law of 1921. This law set an overall **quota**, or limit, of about 358,000 immigrants per year. No more than 20 percent of a nation's yearly quota would be admitted in one month.

At the beginning of each month, ships raced to New York Harbor, hoping to get their passengers through. Sometimes the monthly quota was already filled. Then, people, who may have sold their homes and possessions for a ship's ticket, were turned back.

On July 1, 1922, the steamship Conte Russo sped into New York Harbor. After the First Quota Law of 1921, hopeful immigrants needed to arrive early to be included in the monthly quota.

Henry Curran, commissioner of Ellis Island in 1923, wrote about watching these immigrants depart. "Day by day the barges took them from Ellis Island back to the ships again, back to the ocean, back to what?" Some were carrying little American flags. Some were dressed up in their finest clothing "to celebrate their first glad day in free America." Most, he noticed, were softly weeping. "They twisted something in my heart that hurts to this day."

By the mid-1920s, immigration was greatly reduced from that of the late 1800s. Here, immigrants are shown on the Lower East Side of New York City in 1890.

Even stricter laws were set by the Immigration Act of 1924. Total annual immigration was cut by about half to 164,677. The 1924 law also required immigrants to be examined, inspected, and approved in their native countries. American offices called **consulates** would supervise the process. This would prevent people from traveling thousands of miles only to be sent back. An Ellis Island official who recommended the change explained that it would save thousands of immigrants "the suffering we see at the Island daily, which is indescribable and that would melt a heart of granite."

By 1931, all of the overseas consulates were in place.

Here, the Registry Room, shown in 1954, has been cleared of furniture shortly before Ellis Island is shut down.

WAR SERVICE

During World War I few immigrants entered the United States because it was dangerous to travel overseas. Still, Ellis Island was not empty. The station held German and Austrian sailors captured in American harbors. Wounded American soldiers filled Ellis Island hospitals. Sailors also stayed on Ellis Island while waiting for their ships.

Now, immigrants were brought to Ellis Island only in special cases. There might be a child traveling alone, someone who got sick on the ship, or a foreign criminal who was caught trying to slip in.

In the year between June 1932 and June 1933, only about four thousand people were held at Ellis Island. Contrast this with one day—April 17, 1907—when the Ellis Island staff processed almost twelve thousand immigrants. An official inspecting Ellis Island in 1924 reported that the station looked like a "deserted village." Finally, in 1954 the once bustling station closed.

Today, Ellis Island is preserved as part of the Statue of Liberty National Monument.

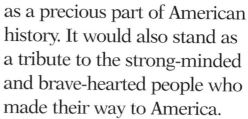

Visitors to the museum can use computers to research photos and ships' passenger records.

Ellis Island's doorway did not stay closed forever. In 1965, President Lyndon Johnson made the former inspection station a national monument. As a national monument, Ellis Island would be preserved as a precious part of American history. It would also stand as a tribute to the strong-minded and brave-hearted people who made their way to America.

In 1990, the immigration station became the Ellis Island Immigration Museum. Exhibits, movies, and photographs record six decades of history. Visitors discover the stories of parents and grandparents who came in search of their future. The immigrants return too—but now they come in search of their past.

One eighty-year-old woman returned to Ellis Island in 1990. Again she became a ten-year-old child, climbing the wide steps into the towering station. She could see the worried faces. She could hear shouts and cries. She could feel the crowds and the confusion. Though seventy years had passed, it all came back to her.

ORAL HISTORY PROJECT

A fascinating section of the Immigration Museum is the Ellis Island Oral History Library. The Oral History Project began in 1973, when interviews with immigrants were tape-recorded and written down. More than twelve hundred people shared their experiences. Although many have since died, the Oral History Library preserves their memories. All of the words of the immigrants in this book were gathered from this American treasure.

The Immigration Museum tells the stories of the many immigrants who passed through its gates.

Timeline: Ellis Island

1890	1891	1892	1897	1900	1907	1917

Congress chooses Ellis Island as the site for New York's federal immigration station.

The Immigration Act of 1891 creates the federal Bureau of Immigration, which sets up an inspection system.

The immigration station opens on Ellis Island on January 1.

A mysterious fire destroys the immigration station on June 14.

The Ellis Island Immigration Station reopens on December 17.

Almost 900,000 immigrants pass through Ellis Island.

The Immigration Act of 1917 requires all immigrants sixteen years and older to be able to read in their native language.

1921 1924 1954 1965 1976 1983 1990

Quota Law of 1921 limits immigration to 357,803 per year, with no more than 155,000 from southern and eastern Europe.

The Immigration Act of 1924 limits immigration to 164,677 per year, allowing fewer than 25,000 from southern and eastern Europe.

The Ellis Island Immigration Station closes in November.

President Lyndon Johnson makes Ellis Island a part of the Statue of Liberty National Monument.

Ellis Island opens for National Park Service tours.

Restoration of Ellis Island begins.

The Ellis Island Immigration Museum opens on September 10.

★ ★ ★ ★

CHAPTER 4

MOUNT RUSHMORE

ANDREW SANTELLA

★ ★ ★ ★

The Mount Rushmore National Memorial honors four of the greatest United States presidents. It is also a monument to the vision of one dedicated artist.

Mount Rushmore National Memorial is one of South Dakota's most-visited sites.

Gutzon Borglum

The memorial is one of the world's most spectacular pieces of sculpture. It has been called "The Shrine of Democracy." The huge likenesses of George Washington, Thomas Jefferson, Abraham Lincoln, and Theodore Roosevelt are carved into the granite wall of Mount Rushmore. The work was designed by the American sculptor Gutzon Borglum. Over fourteen years, he and his son directed the painstaking labor that went into creating the memorial. Against daunting odds, Borglum and his team created an awe-inspiring monument that will endure through the ages.

Borglum and his team blasted 8 million pounds (4 million kilograms) of stone off the mountainside to complete the sculpture. Each of the four faces carved into the mountain is 60 feet (18 meters) long. Borglum's artistry combined with the rugged natural beauty of the Black Hills of South Dakota to create a stunning scene. The memorial is one of the most recognizable sites in the world.

The memorial's story begins in the early 1920s when a South Dakota historian named Doane Robinson first suggested that a huge monument be built in the Black Hills. Robinson knew that South Dakota's Black Hills region was one of the most scenic in the country. He wanted others to know it, too. What the area needed, he believed, was a special attraction to draw visitors.

At around the same time, Gutzon Borglum was in Georgia, working on just the kind of project that Robinson had in mind. Borglum was chiseling the gigantic images of Southern heroes of the Civil War into a Georgia mountainside. Robinson heard about Borglum's Georgia project and wondered if something similar could be done in South Dakota. He knew that this was the kind of project that would attract the nation's attention. And, if it was ever completed, it would be sure to attract visitors.

In 1924, he wrote a letter to Gutzon Borglum. Robinson invited him to visit the Black Hills, look over the area, and decide if he could create a huge work of art there.

The natural beauty of the Black Hills region inspired Doane Robinson to draw visitors to the area.

Robinson could not have made a better choice. Borglum's parents had come to the United States from Denmark. Borglum himself was born in Idaho in 1867. He grew up in Nebraska, but left to study in California when he was seventeen years old. He studied painting in San Francisco and then in Paris, France. Soon, he devoted himself exclusively to sculpture. He moved to England, where his reputation grew. His work made him an internationally known artist. But it was Borglum's work in the United States that made Robinson contact him.

In 1901, one of Borglum's works became the first piece of American sculpture purchased by the Metropolitan Museum of Art in New York. In 1909, Borglum sculpted a bust of Abraham Lincoln that is now in the Capitol Rotunda in Washington, D.C. It was a huge sculpture, carved from a 6-ton block of marble. That led to work on an even grander scale. By 1915, Borglum began working on his enormous memorial carved into the side of Stone Mountain in Georgia. Borglum never finished that project. A dispute with his patrons caused him to resign. But Doane Robinson took note that Borglum was an artist who was willing to take on the challenge of sculpting the side of a mountain.

Ancient Egyptians and Mesopotamians had made similar works thousands of years earlier. They cut enormous statues out of natural rock

114

formations. Borglum wanted to create works of art that were just as massive and impressive. He believed that colossal art was "soul-stirring."

Borglum was known as an artist who thought big. His plans for the Stone Mountain memorial were ambitious. In fact, Borglum was so committed to his vision that many found him difficult to work with. His uncompromising attitude led to problems on the Stone Mountain job. When he didn't get to finish the project, he was bitterly disappointed. He also became more determined than ever to complete a mammoth memorial. If he couldn't do it at Stone Mountain, he would do it elsewhere.

Georgia's Stone Mountain is a memorial to Southern leaders of the Civil War (from left): Jefferson Davis, Robert E. Lee, and Stonewall Jackson.

As Borglum's fame spread, he received more and more offers to do large sculptures. He considered many opportunities, but only one seemed right to him. Something attracted Borglum to the Black Hills of South Dakota. Maybe it was Borglum's background as the son of western pioneers. All his life, Borglum promoted the virtues of his native land. When the chance came to do a massive work of art in the American West, he could hardly pass it up.

His first visit to the Black Hills made him even more enthusiastic. In September 1924, Borglum came to South Dakota to meet with Robinson. At

Red Cloud declared war on the U.S. government for building forts in Sioux territory.

that time, Robinson didn't have in mind a monument to presidents. He was thinking of honoring great figures from the American West. He had proposed the explorers Meriwether Lewis and William Clark or the Oglala Sioux leader Red Cloud. Lewis and Clark gained fame for their 1804–06 expedition of the Louisiana Purchase, from St. Louis, Missouri, to present-day Astoria, Oregon, and back. Red Cloud was an American-Indian warrior and chief. During the 1860s, Red Cloud led raids on U.S. Army forts in Wyoming and Montana that had been built in Sioux territory. In 1868, the army abandoned the forts.

As a result, Red Cloud is known as the only American Indian who ever won a war against the U.S. government.

Later it was decided to build a memorial to great presidents. Robinson didn't have Mount Rushmore itself in mind as the site for the monument. He considered several other places in the Black Hills for the project. One of those areas was the Needles, a series of jagged, rugged peaks. It was the first place Robinson and Borglum visited. The two men rode horses for miles over the rugged terrain. Borglum was amazed at the beauty of the jagged peaks. The views were stunning. Rock formations jutted skyward. Deep canyons split the pine forests. Trout flourished in clear streams and wildlife teemed in the woods. "Here is the place," Borglum said to Robinson. "American history shall march along that skyline."

Robinson and Borglum first considered the Needles region of South Dakota as the place to establish a monument.

* * * *

As it turned out, the irregular peaks of the Needles were too badly weathered to stand up to carving. But that didn't discourage Borglum. Later on the trip, he told a South Dakota audience, "I know of no grouping of rock formations that equals those found in the Black Hills . . . nor any that is so suitable to sculpture." Finishing with a flourish, he called the hills a "garden of the gods." Borglum was still thinking big. He wanted the residents of the area to think big right along with him.

It wasn't until the next year (1925), though, that Borglum settled on the site for his work. It was an enormous mountain. Its main wall was almost 500 feet (152 m) long, large enough for the work he had in mind. It towered over the other nearby peaks, making it visible from a

Mount Rushmore in 1925, before the project began

distance. The granite sides of the mountain were stable enough to stand up to carving. The walls loomed above slopes of wildflowers and timber. Best of all, the mountain faced southeast, giving it exposure to sunlight. It was known to locals as Mount Rushmore. On its surface, Borglum would etch his grand vision.

One day in August 1925, Borglum and his son Lincoln set out with a small group to climb Mount Rushmore. It was their first trip up the mountain that would be the center of their lives for years to come. It was a grueling climb. In some places, the group had to scale walls that went straight up. But everyone in the group made it to the top of the cliff—even the 58-year-old sculptor and his 13-year-old son.

Gutzon Borglum (second from right) and the members of his party prepare to leave the town of Keystone, South Dakota, for their first climb up Mount Rushmore. (Lincoln Borglum is standing next to his father.)

George Washington

Thomas Jefferson

Abraham Lincoln

Theodore Roosevelt

Difficult as it was, the climb was well worth it. The views from the top were stunning. Borglum and the others could see mile after mile of mountains and plains stretching into the distance—west into Wyoming, east to the plains of South Dakota. Later Borglum wrote that he felt like he was in another world. It was then that he decided that "plans must change. The vastness I saw here demanded it." Once again, Borglum's plans were getting bigger, his vision grander.

Borglum decided that he couldn't limit himself to a monument to heroes of the Old West. Instead, he decided the site called for a "great American memorial"—one that honored the giants of American history. Before long, the sculptor was drawing sketches of George Washington and Abraham Lincoln. Soon he was including Thomas Jefferson, as well. And as he realized how much room he had to work with on the massive mountain, Borglum grew even bolder. "Here we have such stone large enough for not one but three or four or five figures," he wrote.

Borglum wanted the memorial to tell the story of the United States. His idea was to pay tribute to the presidents who saw the nation through its founding, its growth, its preservation and its development. In a speech in Rapid City, he declared that the figures carved into the mountain were "to be those of George

★ ★ ★ ★

Washington, Thomas Jefferson, Abraham Lincoln, and Theodore Roosevelt."

Washington served as the first president of the United States, from 1789 to 1797. Jefferson doubled the size of the United States with the Louisiana Purchase and was the country's third president, from 1801 to 1809. Lincoln, who insured the preservation of the Union during the Civil War, served as the sixteenth president, from 1861 to 1865. And Roosevelt, representing the United States's development as a powerful nation, was the twenty-sixth president, from 1901 to 1909.

Borglum worked in his studio at the base of Mount Rushmore to turn his sketches into plaster models before they were actually carved into the mountain.

Although Borglum's masterpiece was already taking shape in his mind, he still wasn't sure it could really be done. He had taken great care in choosing Mount Rushmore for his work. But until he began sculpting, he couldn't know if the mountain held some flaw that would ruin his work. It was weather-beaten and aged. It had stood in the heart of the Black Hills for millions of years. It showed its age.

Long before Borglum carved it, wind and rain had already etched its face. Mount Rushmore's cliff wall has been described as looking like elephant skin—gray and wrinkled. It was lined

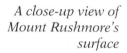

A close-up view of Mount Rushmore's surface

with crevices. Borglum had to take these crevices into consideration in designing his monument. But at least he could see them. Until he began carving, he had no way of knowing the condition of the stone inside the cliff. Would it be too hard to cut? Would it be too brittle? Would there be flaws in the stone that would mar his monument?

Borglum could not answer any of these questions until he began cutting into the face of Mount Rushmore. Still, he did not let doubts delay him. He forged ahead, certain that Rushmore was the right place for the memorial. But first he had to convince others that Mount Rushmore was the wise choice. Senator Peter Norbeck of South Dakota had been involved in the project since its earliest stages. He was willing to take Borglum's word that Rushmore offered the best sculpting surface. But what about other considerations? For one thing, the remote cliff was far from good roads. And roads would certainly be needed to move workers and haul equipment to and from the site.

Senator Peter Norbeck

Borglum did not let the senator's objections slow him. He was itching to begin work on the mountain. He even announced that he planned to dedicate the site in October 1925. That was news to Senator Norbeck. "This man works so fast," wrote the senator, "that it is hard . . . even to keep track of him."

★   ★   ★   ★

There was one detail that still needed to be worked out, however. Who was going to pay for the work on Mount Rushmore? Borglum had already promised the people of South Dakota that they would not pay the bill for the memorial. But he never said exactly how it would be paid for. A group of Rapid City merchants bailed Borglum out temporarily when they began a fundraising drive to cover some of the initial fees. Much more money would be needed, though.

One thing that was not lacking at this point was the support of the area population. As Dedication Day (October 1, 1925) neared, excitement about the memorial grew. Locals pitched in to make sure the dedication went off smoothly. A women's group stitched five huge American flags, 18 feet (5 m) wide by 30 feet (9 m) long. Men from the town of Keystone used their own axes and shovels to clear a road to Mount Rushmore. And on the big day itself, some three thousand people gathered to see Borglum and Senator Norbeck dedicate the memorial. The sculptor promised that work on the image of George Washington would be done within a year. "Meet me here a year from today and we will dedicate it," he told the cheering crowd.

Borglum didn't meet that deadline. He didn't even come close. But he and his supporters

slowly made progress. A local fund-raising drive netted its goal of $25,000. The national and state legislation needed for the completion of the project was passed. The state built a road to Mount Rushmore. And, in 1927, the Black Hills received a famous visitor. President Calvin Coolidge came to vacation near Mount Rushmore for three months. Borglum did not pass up the chance for publicity that the president's visit offered. On August 10, 1927, he dedicated Mount Rushmore again.

Part of the crowd at the first dedication, which was held on October 1, 1925

The second dedication was a lot like the first. There were speeches and a flag-raising ceremony. But this time, the president of the United States was there. His presence gave even greater importance to the event. Coolidge wore cowboy boots and a western hat and he listened to Borglum talk about his project. The sculptor called it "a memorial to the first modern republic in the western world." Then Borglum was lowered in a harness and drilled the first holes in the side of the mountain. Now the task of actually building the memorial was at long last about to begin.

Borglum's crew operated from a

Above: President Calvin Coolidge, speaking at the second dedication of Mount Rushmore

Right: Workers stand atop Mount Rushmore. The lines on the mountainside indicate places Borglum has marked off to begin carving.

★ ★ ★ ★

base called Doane Mountain, named for Doane Robinson, located across a gulch from Mount Rushmore. By fall, the base was a cluster of buildings including a blacksmith shop, a bunkhouse, a restaurant, and a studio for the sculptor. The base was connected to Mount Rushmore by a cable that supported a large steel bucket loaded with supplies. The cableway was not safe enough for the crew, though. Instead, they had to walk up hundreds of stairs every day to get to their work stations. It was the equivalent of walking up a forty-story building.

The restaurant building at the workers' base camp

★ ★ ★ ★

The workers' first task was to measure a rough outline for the head of George Washington. Then they could begin peeling away the stone to get to the clean surface that would be sculpted. Borglum's crew did their work suspended from the top of the mountain in swings. Dangling in mid-air, they used jackhammers to drill holes in the side of the mountain and chip away at it. This took so long that soon Borglum was ready to try another solution. In late October, they began blasting away rock with dynamite. Eventually about 500,000 tons of stone was blasted off the mountain. The figure of Washington was the first to be completed. It was not ready for unveiling until 1930.

Workers lower themselves onto the rock's surface to begin work on the head of George Washington.

＊　＊　＊　＊

But an even larger problem was looming. Funds for the project were running low. In 1928, no work at all was done on the monument. It took the support of the federal government to get work on Mount Rushmore started again. Senator Norbeck and South Dakota Congressman William Williamson introduced legislation to provide federal funding. Their bill called for the government to pay for half the cost of the memorial, up to $250,000. The funding would not be direct, though. It would come in the form of "matching funds." That is, the government would contribute one dollar for every dollar raised from private sources. It was signed into law by President Coolidge on February 25, 1929.

In July 1929, the Mount Rushmore National Memorial Commission visited the site to check on the work's progress. (In the front row are pictured Doane Robinson, second from left, and Gutzon Borglum, fourth from left.)

In this photograph, taken several years into the project, Borglum travels on the cableway from the camp to the mountain to direct the carving.

The law's passage meant that work on Mount Rushmore could resume. But it didn't solve all the financial problems. In 1929, not long after the Mount Rushmore law was passed, the stock market crashed and the nation fell into the Great Depression. Banks closed, ordinary people lost their jobs, and the entire national economy was in peril. Under such circumstances, private funds for the monument were scarce. And if little money could be raised from private sources, just as little would come from the government.

Over the next few years, financial problems would plague the Mount Rushmore operation. A regular supply of money was needed to pay workers and to keep equipment running. Every so often, money would run low and work would have to stop. Then a new source of funds would be discovered and work would start up again—

until the next crisis. The situation made the project a very lengthy one. It wasn't until 1934 that the problem was solved. That year, the Mount Rushmore legislation was changed to provide for direct appropriation. That meant there was a steady supply of money flowing to keep the work going.

But even with financial problems solved, the weather could still cause trouble. When temperatures dipped down around 0 degrees Fahrenheit (18 degrees Celsius), or when rain or snow was severe, work stopped. Eventually Borglum had temporary shelters set up on the sides of the mountains to protect his workers from the elements.

Shelters on the mountain protected workers from the harsh effects of the weather.

Most of the workers on the mountain were local men. Some had been miners or ranchers or lumbermen. Many were struggling to make ends meet during the Depression. At Mount Rushmore, they found work they could believe in. The hours were long and the work was hard. But most were proud to be working on a project of such importance. Depending on how much money was available, as many as seventy workers might be toiling on the mountain at once. In leaner times, there might be only a handful at work.

They started work at 7:30 A.M. with a long climb to the top of Mount Rushmore. Workmen were lowered to their assigned stations to drill holes in the surface of the mountain. Then they filled the holes with explosive powder. They ignited the powder twice a day—at lunchtime and at the end of the day. The blasts echoed through the hills and canyons around Mount Rushmore. Granite came crashing down the mountainside by the ton.

As the cutting got closer to the actual sculpting surface, workers had to be more careful. They used air-powered tools to remove the last few inches

A huge flag beside the head of George Washington commemorates its 1930 dedication.

of stone. Then more was broken off with hammers and wedges. Finally, the gleaming, solid rock underneath was exposed and ready for careful carving. The last, most precise cuts were made with hand chisels. Borglum observed from different angles and distances. He examined the work at various times of the day and night. He studied the way light and shadow played over the figures. Then he provided the final touches that gave the work life and feeling.

In this 1935 photograph, sculptors continue work on the face of George Washington.

One by one, the figures were completed. Washington was completed in 1930. Jefferson was unveiled in 1936. Lincoln followed in 1937, the 150th anniversary of the U.S. Constitution. Finally, Theodore Roosevelt was unveiled in 1939. It was nine years after the head of Washington had been completed, and fourteen years after Gutzon Borglum had first climbed Mount Rushmore.

President Franklin Delano Roosevelt attended the dedication of the Thomas Jefferson figure on August 30, 1936. His words that day make it clear that the memorial had a profound impact on him. "I had seen the photographs, I had seen

When the head of Thomas Jefferson was unveiled in 1936, work on the heads of Lincoln (covered by the flag) and Roosevelt was well under way.

Beneath the emerging face of Abraham Lincoln, the tons of granite that were blasted away from the mountain are clearly visible.

Although not yet completed, Roosevelt's head (surrounded by scaffolding) was unveiled on July 3, 1939.

the drawings, and I had talked with those who are responsible for this great work," he said. "And yet I had no conception, until about ten minutes ago, not only of its magnitude, but also of its permanent beauty and importance."

★　★　★　★

A final dedication of the monument was planned for 1941. But Gutzon Borglum would not survive that long. He died on a trip to Chicago, Illinois, that year, the result of a minor operation. The sculptor of Mount Rushmore was seventy-four. He didn't live long enough to see his sculpture completed. But he did live long enough to see his vision realized. He saw the images of America's great presidents emerge from the granite of the Black Hills of South Dakota.

Fittingly, Gutzon Borglum's son saw the project through to its close. After Gutzon Borglum's death, the Mount Rushmore workmen signed a petition asking that Lincoln Borglum be allowed to finish his father's work. Lincoln Borglum saw that the last details of the monument were completed.

In this 1941 photograph, Lincoln Borglum descends the mountainside to complete the finishing touches on the face of Abraham Lincoln.

There was plenty of work left for Lincoln Borglum to do. Details of the heads were still incomplete. The hair of each president had to be sculpted. And the rubble from years of blasting had to be cleared from the mountain. Lincoln Borglum did as much of this work as he could in the months following his father's death. But World War II (1939–45) was approaching. Once the United States was involved in that all-out

* * * *

effort, there would be precious little manpower or resources for the project on Mount Rushmore.

Work on the mountain shut down in October 1941 and never started again. In one sense, the sculpting work on Mount Rushmore was never completed. On the other hand, the figures on Mount Rushmore will remain for ages to come. They stand as an example of the sculptor's art, as a tribute to the will of the sculptor himself, and as a memorial to the presidents of a great nation.

On July 3, 1991, President George Bush spoke during the fiftieth anniversary celebration of Mount Rushmore.

TIMELINE

1867 Gutzon Borglum born in Idaho

1901 Borglum's work purchased by
Metropolitan Museum of Art in New York

Borglum sculpts figure of Abraham **1909**
Lincoln, now in U.S. Capitol

1915 Borglum works on Stone Mountain
in Georgia

1924 Doane Robinson writes to Gutzon Borglum

1925

President Calvin Coolidge visits Black Hills **1927**

Figure of George Washington unveiled **1930**

Figure of Thomas Jefferson unveiled **1936**
Figure of Abraham Lincoln unveiled **1937**
Figure of Theodore Roosevelt unveiled **1939**

Gutzon Borglum dies; work continued **1941**
by Lincoln Borglum

Borglum
makes first
trip to Mount
Rushmore

★ ★ ★ ★

CHAPTER 5

THE STATUE OF LIBERTY

ELAINE LANDAU

October 28, 1886, was a damp, chilly day in New York City. A cold wind swept over New York Harbor, hinting that a freezing winter was on its way. Yet that didn't stop a large crowd from gathering for an event that had been years in the making. In addition, more than three hundred boats had arrived in the harbor for the occasion. Their crisp white sails formed a patchwork against the choppy gray water.

What began as a gift of international friendship would soon become an enduring symbol of freedom and democracy.

On land, New York City's mayor and the state governor began to take their seats. United States President Grover Cleveland also arrived to give the speech of the day. Nevertheless, none of these officials was the star of the event. The excitement was not about a person, but a statue. Everyone was there for the **dedication** of a huge **monument** named

"Liberty Enlightening the World," more commonly known today as the Statue of Liberty.

The 151-foot (46-meter) copper structure was indeed a magnificent sight. Taking the form of the Roman goddess of Liberty—Libertas—the statue holds a torch lighting the way to liberty. The broken shackles at the statue's feet stand for freedom from **tyranny**. The law tablet in her left hand represents the Declaration of Independence and the American ideal that "all men are created equal."

Surrounded by symbols of patriotism, President Grover Cleveland spoke to a cheering crowd at the dedication of the Statue of Liberty in October, 1886.

HER CROWNING GLORY

Lady Liberty, as the statue is sometimes called, is more than just a **hollow** form—she has an **interior** that people can enter. Stairs lead to the top of the statue and to the twenty-five windows set in her crown. Many people think that the crown's seven points, or rays, represent the seven seas and seven continents of the world. However, they are actually meant to form a halo, as a reminder that the sculpture is divine, or holy.

The statue was a gift from France to the United States symbolizing the bond of friendship between the two nations. However, in time it would come to mean much more. The Statue of Liberty would become an enduring symbol of freedom and democracy to Americans and people around the world.

Praising the statue on behalf of the nation, President Grover Cleveland said, "We will not forget that Liberty has made here her home; nor shall her chosen altar be neglected." The statue's dedication was heralded by a twenty-one-gun salute, followed later that evening with a spectacular ball. Everything was perfect.

Twenty-two flights of stairs lead to the statue's crown. Some visitors prefer a shorter trip—192 steps or an elevator—to the pedestal observation deck, which also offers a good view of New York Harbor.

★ ★ ★ ★

The road to creating the Statue of Liberty, however, was far from perfect. It all began at a dinner party in France in 1865. The party, hosted by French historian and politician Professor Édouard-René de Laboulaye, was attended by an assortment of French statesmen and intellectuals. Among the guests was Frédéric-Auguste Bartholdi, a thirty-one-year-old sculptor who was a highly respected member of the art world.

During a lively discussion at dinner Laboulaye remarked on the significant friendship between France and the United States. During the American Revolution,

French sculptor Frédéric-Auguste Bartholdi would spend many years working on the Statue of Liberty, which would later be considered one of his best works.

AN OUTSTANDING ARTIST

Frédéric-Auguste Bartholdi was born on August 2, 1834, in Alsace, France. Bartholdi's mother, Charlotte, recognized his creative genius early on and encouraged her son's interest in art. While at first Bartholdi studied painting, he later became more interested in sculpture. Besides the Statue of Liberty, Bartholdi's other sculptures in the United States include the Bartholdi Fountain in the Botanic Garden in Washington, D.C. (left), and the Lafayette statue in New York City. He died in Paris on October 4, 1904, of tuberculosis.

Many people in France sympathized with the American cause for independence from Great Britain, leading the country to take up arms on behalf of the American colonists.

France had proved itself a valuable ally by supporting the American colonists in their fight for independence from Great Britain. It sent both funds and supplies to the colonists, and at times, French soldiers had fought alongside them, as well. A number of the colonists' victories may not have been possible without the help of the French fleet and army; therefore, France was instrumental in enabling the colonists to establish a government based on freedom and liberty. Laboulaye, as well as many others, longed to see a similar form of democracy in France. In a democracy the people choose their leaders in elections.

But Napoleon III, who was the emperor of France at the time, would never allow this.

Laboulaye felt a "genuine flow of sympathy" between France and the United States and described the countries as "two sisters." Aware that the hundredth anniversary of the colonists' independence was just eleven years away, Laboulaye hoped to give the United States a special hundredth birthday present on behalf of France.

He decided that the gift should be a monument honoring liberty. Laboulaye explained that this monument would have a **dual** purpose. It would reinforce France's bond with America. In addition, the gift would stress to Napoleon III's regime that the French people were dedicated to the concept of liberty and equality.

Bartholdi wrote that the seed for the Statue of Liberty was sown at the party that night. It is generally thought that Laboulaye's opinion influenced Bartholdi, who began thinking along the same lines. Nevertheless, actual plans for the monument did not begin for years. In July 1870, France

THE FRIENDSHIP CONTINUED

Even after the American Revolution the bond between France and the United States remained strong. The French were greatly saddened by President Abraham Lincoln's **assassination** in 1865. They felt that an important defender of equality was gone forever, as they had respected the stand he took against slavery. To show their sympathy, the people of France gave Mrs. Lincoln a gold medal with an **inscription** in French:

Dedicated by French democracy to Lincoln, twice-elected President of the United States—honest Lincoln who abolished slavery, reestablished the union, and saved the Republic, without veiling the Statue of Liberty.

Édouard-René de Laboulaye proposed the building of a memorial to honor the bond between France and the United States.

149

★　★　★　★

declared war on Germany and the Franco-Prussian War began. Bartholdi served in the French Army, and art took a backseat as the sculptor fought for his country. By 1871 the war had ended, and Napoleon III had fallen.

Bartholdi is shown here in his studio in Paris around 1892. He favored large-scale sculptures and worked from small models.

Laboulaye and Bartholdi hoped that the time might be right for democracy to take root in France. They thought that creating the statue now might encourage others to see the value of such a system. Bartholdi is quoted as saying: "I will try to

★ ★ ★ ★

glorify the Republic and Liberty over there [in the United States] in the hope that someday I will find it again here."

At first no one was sure what form the statue would take, but one thing was certain: If Bartholdi designed it, the monument was bound to be big. Nearly all of Bartholdi's pieces were created on a grand scale. Many people believed that the sculptor had been greatly influenced by what he saw when he visited Egypt. Impressed by the size of such structures as the pyramids and the Sphinx, Bartholdi longed for a sense of massiveness in his own work. His first public monument—**commissioned** when he was just eighteen—was a 12-foot (3.7-m) high statue of one of Napoleon's generals. Workmen had barely been able to remove the larger-than-life sculpture from Bartholdi's studio. Yet the work received a good deal of praise and helped establish its creator's reputation as an artist.

Bartholdi was excited about doing a sculpture for the United States. To explore how the Americans would feel about it, Bartholdi headed for the U.S.

This illustration (below) shows a bird's eye view of New York Harbor, from lower Manhattan. Bartholdi said that the idea for Lady Liberty became clear when he got his first view of the harbor.

★ ★ ★ ★

In the years following its dedication, the statue had an overwhelming impact on immigrants arriving in New York. In the words of one person, ". . . she represented the big, powerful country that was to be our future home."

in the summer of 1871. He hoped to drum up enthusiasm for the project as well as find an appealing location to display the work. Bartholdi spent most of his days on the voyage making sketches of different views of Lady Liberty. The sculptor had also brought along a small model of the proposed monument to give Americans a better idea of how the finished product would look.

Bartholdi did not have to look very far to find the perfect spot for Lady Liberty. He spied the ideal place for her as soon as his ship entered New York Harbor. It was Bedloe's Island, one of a group of small islands in the harbor. At one time, the Mohegan Indians had called the island Minnissais, which

Bedloe's Island, an abandoned military post, was chosen as the future home for the Statue of Liberty.

LIBERTY'S HOME

Congress approved Bedloe's Island as the home for Lady Liberty on February 22, 1877. The little island had once belonged to a Dutch man named Isaac Bedloe, but by 1877 it was in the hands of the U.S. government. Much later, on August 3, 1956, the site's name would be changed to Liberty Island.

means "Lesser Island," because it was so small. Despite its small size, the island seemed perfect for the project because New York Harbor was an active seaport where this tribute to liberty would get the attention it deserved. The French sculptor further described the location as a place "where people [immigrants] get their first view of the New World." He wanted them to see the statue before anything else.

Finding a suitable site for the monument was just one phase of Bartholdi's mission. Creating a sense of enthusiasm for the statue among Americans proved to be much more difficult. Laboulaye had supplied the young sculptor with letters of introduction to a number of important Americans. Bartholdi met with President Ulysses S. Grant and American literary figures, including Henry Wadsworth Longfellow, to talk about the project.

154

Although Bartholdi managed to pique the curiosity of some Americans, few appeared very enthusiastic. While the statue was to be a gift from the French, Americans would have to help finance it. Most of the people Bartholdi spoke to were not especially anxious to part with their money to make his dream come true. When Bartholdi returned to France, both he and Laboulaye agreed that they were not ready to begin construction.

This photograph features Bartholdi's first model of the statue's head, made of bronze.

The two Frenchmen made another attempt to get financial backing for the monument in 1874. They proposed dividing the cost of the monument between France and the United States. France would pay for the statue itself, while America was to pay for its pedestal and foundation. To speed things along, in 1875 Laboulaye formed the Franco-American Union, which included people from France as well as the United States. This organization worked to bring in **donations** on both sides of the Atlantic.

Though the original goal of completing the statue for the hundredth birthday (July 4, 1876) of the United States seemed unlikely, the group still did its best to meet that deadline. Appeals for donations for the statue appeared in the French press by the fall of 1875. The Franco-American Union proved quite creative in its fund-raising efforts. Banquets and balls were held in several French cities. The food and ballrooms for these occasions were donated, and all admission fees went to the statue's fund. Bartholdi came up with just enough money to begin work on Lady Liberty.

PICTURE THIS

Lady Liberty is a really big statue:

- Each of her hands is 150 square feet (14 square meters), or about the size of a small classroom.

- Her index finger is about 8 feet (2.4 m) long, or about the size of a female tiger.

- Each of her fingernails is about the size of a spiral notebook.

- She weighs 225 tons (229 metric tons), which almost equals the weight of forty-five African elephants.

Creating such a large sculpture was a tremendous undertaking. Bartholdi worked with a wide range of craftsmen. Metalsmiths were essential in creating the statue's framework and **exterior**. Carpenters, plasterers, painters, and others were needed to build the statue's "walk-in" interior.

It was crucial that the best material be selected for the statue's construction. Both stone and bronze seemed like good choices for Lady Liberty, but neither was right for the task. They were both too heavy to ship across the Atlantic.

In the end, copper was chosen. Copper is light, easy to work with, and strong enough to withstand the rough sea voyage to America. It was also thought that the material was less likely to be damaged by the salty-air environment of New York Harbor. At first, the statue would be a shiny orange-brown color, like a piece of new copper piping. In time, however, exposure to the elements would turn the copper an attractive blue-green color, which would blend in well with the harbor landscape.

A tremendous amount of work went into the statue's construction. Workmen hammered and pressed thin sheets of copper into shape using a series of increasingly larger molds, so that the statue grew larger as additional layers were added. More than three hundred individual copper sheets were needed to create Lady Liberty's outer form. Due to its immense size, the statue was made in hundreds of smaller segments and held together by rivets, or strong metal bolts.

Large numbers of French craftsmen were employed to build the Statue of Liberty. Only small portions of the statue could be worked on at a time.

* * * *

Carpenters made wooden molds of each section, onto which copper sheets were pressed and hammered.

An engineer was hired to work with Bartholdi in designing a strong skeletal, or inner, framework to support the statue. This was vital because the statue was expected to last for centuries. The person selected for this job was a highly respected structural engineer named Gustave Eiffel. Known as the Magician of Iron, Eiffel had been extremely

158

innovative in using iron to build a number of large bridges. Now he turned his attention to devising a huge iron skeleton for Lady Liberty.

Gustave Eiffel was a talented engineer who, at the time, was primarily known for designing bridges.

QUITE A TOWER

In 1889, Gustave Eiffel would become famous for designing the Eiffel Tower (left) in Paris, France—one of the best known landmarks in the world. The Eiffel Tower has nearly six million visitors each year. Maintenance teams are always busy keeping the tower clean because it is so big. Each year, they use 4 tons of paper towels and 25,000 garbage bags, as well as many other cleaning supplies.

A portion of the statue's arm and the torch were displayed at the International Centennial Exhibition in Philadelphia. The exhibition, held in celebration of the country's hundredth birthday, was a tribute to the great strides made in science, industry, and international relations.

*   *   *   *

Bartholdi was not able to complete the statue in time for America's centennial, or hundredth birthday. But the statue's raised arm and torch were finished by the summer of 1876. This portion of the statue was shipped to the United States to give Americans a taste of what was to come. The piece arrived just as the International Centennial Exhibition in Philadelphia, Pennsylvania, was taking place, so it was exhibited there. The statue's 30-foot (9.1-m) arm and torch were quite a hit, as most visitors had never seen a piece of sculpture that was large enough to hold a group of people inside.

Bartholdi's mother, shown here, was the model for the statue's face.

Following the Philadelphia exposition, the arm and torch were displayed in New York City at Madison Square Park. For just fifty cents each, visitors could climb a ladder inside the statue's arm, which led to the balcony encircling her torch. People enjoyed exploring the oversized sculpture. For the first time, genuine enthusiasm for the statue began to take root in the United States.

Before long, additional parts of the statue were completed. Lady Liberty's shiny copper head was displayed at the Paris Universal Exposition of 1878.

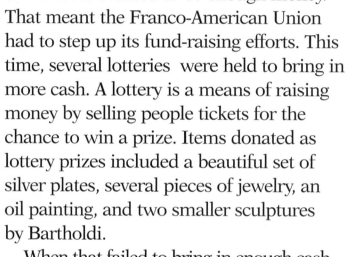

By then Bartholdi had begun calling the sculpture "My daughter, Liberty." However, Bartholdi's mother was actually the model for the statue's face.

Crowds in Paris loved the sculpture. Yet the problem that plagued the project from the start still existed—there never seemed to be enough money.

Modern-day miniatures of the statue are still popular collectibles.

That meant the Franco-American Union had to step up its fund-raising efforts. This time, several lotteries were held to bring in more cash. A lottery is a means of raising money by selling people tickets for the chance to win a prize. Items donated as lottery prizes included a beautiful set of silver plates, several pieces of jewelry, an oil painting, and two smaller sculptures by Bartholdi.

When that failed to bring in enough cash, the Franco-American Union came up with yet another idea. It made small clay miniatures of the statue, which were sold as collectibles. Each model had the Franco-American Union's seal on it, and buyers could get their family's name engraved on the small replica, or copy. The miniatures sold for three thousand dollars (one thousand francs in France) each and were quite popular. At the close of 1879 it looked as if sufficient money might have been raised to finish the statue.

Bartholdi set to work in earnest on the project, and before long, substantial parts of the huge monument began to take shape. In a letter dated December 19, 1882, he wrote to the

As work on the statue advanced, some sections were put on display in Paris, France.

chairman of the American Committee of the Franco-American Union to report on his progress. "Our work advances. The statue commences to reach above the houses, and by next spring we shall see it overlook the entire city, as the large monuments of Paris now do."

On behalf of the United States, Levi P. Morton accepted the statue as a gift in Paris.

The statue was finally completed by June of 1884. On the Fourth of July it was formally presented to Levi P. Morton, the minister of the United States to France. Accepting the gift in Paris on behalf of the American people, Morton said, "God grant that it [the statue] may stand until the end of time as an emblem of imperishable sympathy and affection

The statue was displayed in Paris before being shipped to the United States.

★ ★ ★ ★

STATUE TRIVIA

- Winds of 50 miles per hour (80 kilometers per hour) cause the body of the Statue of Liberty to sway up to 3 inches (7.6 centimeters) while the torch sometimes sways up to 5 inches (12.7 cm). This doesn't mean that the statue is unstable. Buildings and large monuments have traditionally been designed this way to withstand wind.

- It takes 354 steps to reach the crown, and 192 steps to reach the top of the pedestal.

- The twenty-five windows in the crown represent the number of gemstones, or "natural minerals," found on Earth. They also stand for heaven's rays of light shining over the world.

between the Republic of France and the United States." Lady Liberty was displayed in France before being sent to America, and the statue soon began to draw large crowds. Thousands of French citizens came to see it before it was shipped to its final destination in the United States.

Bartholdi and Laboulaye's dream was finally being realized. Sadly, Laboulaye died in 1883, before the statue's completion. But Bartholdi anxiously awaited the day when his masterpiece would be mounted on its pedestal. The French sculptor had no idea, however, that things were not so rosy across the Atlantic.

In fact, while Bartholdi had been putting the final touches on his creation, a vital piece of the project—Lady Liberty's pedestal—remained unfinished.

The delay stemmed from the usual problem—lack of funding. Donations for the Statue of Liberty's pedestal had fallen far below expectations. Many Americans had mixed feelings about the structure, but most felt that its estimated cost was too high.

The statue's promoters tried without success to get the government to pay for it. Congress failed to approve a bill that would have provided one hundred thousand dollars for the pedestal. The state of New York tried to help out by

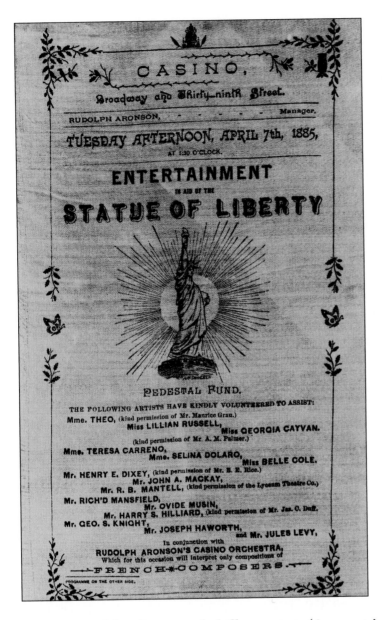

In the United States, theatrical events, art exhibitions, and auctions were some of the events planned to raise money for the statue's pedestal.

allotting a fifty-thousand-dollar grant. (A grant is a sum of money that may be given by the government for a particular purpose.) However, the funds never came through because the governor vetoed, or rejected, it.

Although the Statue of Liberty was to remain permanently in the United States, it was difficult to convince most Americans to donate money to the project. People tended to think of Lady Liberty as a statue belonging to the state of New York rather than a national monument. They argued that New Yorkers should foot the bill. Meanwhile, the price was too steep for New York residents to meet without help.

In response, the American Committee of the Franco-American Union held a number of fund-raisers. They sponsored theatrical events, art shows, auctions, and even prize fights. Unfortunately, these efforts failed to bring in much money. By 1884 things had nearly hit rock bottom. Some wondered if Lady Liberty would ever reach New York Harbor.

It was Joseph Pulitzer, owner of the *New York World* newspaper, who came to the statue's rescue. Pulitzer hoped that he could save the statue and boost his newspaper's circulation at the same time. He printed the following challenge in the *New York World* to urge his readers to act: "The *[New York] World* is the people's paper and now it appeals to the people to come forward and raise the money [for Lady Liberty's pedestal]." Noting that the statue had been paid for by "the masses of the French people," Pulitzer encouraged *New York World* readers to do the same with the statue's pedestal. "Let us respond in like manner. Let us not wait for the millionaires to give this money. It is not a gift from the millionaires of France to the millionaires of America, but a

Joseph Pulitzer, a talented Hungarian-American newspaper publisher, came to the U.S. in 1864. He would later be known for creating the Pulitzer Prize, an award for excellence in journalism, letters, and music.

gift of the whole people of France to the whole people of America." Pulitzer also promised to publish the names of all who gave, no matter how small the donation.

Pulitzer's harsh criticism of those who failed to contribute, published in his newspaper, The New York World, succeeded in raising enough money to complete the pedestal.

The newspaper owner further argued that the Statue of Liberty was not a regional monument but instead stood for ideals common to all Americans. A number of African American newspapers followed the *New York World's* lead in encouraging donations. These publications connected the statue's symbolic message of freedom and liberty with the end of slavery.

Americans heard the call and acted accordingly. The *New York World's* circulation rose by almost fifty thousand readers. Many of these individuals were inspired by Pulitzer's plea. They began donating whatever they could for the cause. Elderly people sent in dollar bills, while children emptied their piggy banks. School classes collected money for the pedestal. By the summer of 1885 Pulitzer's $100,000 goal for the pedestal had been reached. The *New York World* reported that the money was the result of 121,000 individual contributions.

Once financial backing for the statue's pedestal was secured, the project's pace quickened. The architect selected to design the pedestal was a well-known American home designer named Richard Morris Hunt. The **granite** pedestal he created for the statue was built in the center of the eleven-pointed star-shaped walls that had once been part of Fort Wood. Fort Wood had been built on Bedloe's Island in the early 1800s to defend New York against naval attacks. Hunt's 89-foot (27.1-m) pedestal rested on a concrete foundation. To support the massive statue, the foundation

Richard Morris Hunt designed the pedestal. Hunt, who designed mansions for the wealthy, had a reputation for excellence.

The pedestal was built in the center of Fort Wood.

BARTHOLDI.

contained 24,000 tons (24,385 metric tons) of concrete, setting a record for the largest amount of concrete ever poured for a single structure.

Meanwhile, in France the massive undertaking of **dismantling** and packing up the monument was well under way. The statue finally arrived at Bedloe's Island on June 17, 1885. It had been transported from France to the United

A MONUMENTAL TASK

The Statue of Liberty's pedestal is among the heaviest pieces of masonry ever constructed. When it was finally completed on April 22, 1886, the exuberant group of workers tossed their own coins into the **mortar** in celebration.

Crowds of cheering Americans watched as the Isere approached New York Harbor carrying the many pieces of the Statue of Liberty.

States on the French **frigate** *Isere*. The 350 individual pieces of the statue came carefully wrapped and labeled in 214 specially designed wooden crates. Some of the crates weighed just a few hundred pounds, while others weighed several tons. It took several months to uncrate and assemble the pieces of the statue, but it was worth the wait. The finished product was a tremendous source of pride for the country and made everyone's efforts seem worthwhile.

SHINING BRIGHT

The American public liked the idea of having the statue in the harbor, but before long, people noticed that the statue's torch did not shine as far out to sea as intended. That called for a change in Lady Liberty's lighting system. Through the years the statue's lighting would be enhanced a number of times as more technologically advanced equipment was developed. The torch's entire lighting system is equal to 2,500 times the effect of full moonlight.

The statue's lighting, which was a problem from the beginning, has been updated several times with more modern equipment.

In addition to having a formal dedication ceremony on October 28, 1886, more than twenty thousand people took part in a parade that day in honor of this special event. It's estimated that despite rainy weather, more than one million people came out to see the marchers. Everyone was excited about the statue.

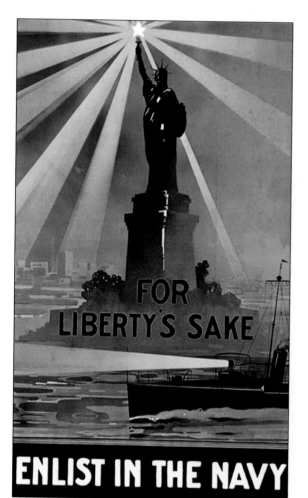

FOR LIBERTY'S SAKE

ENLIST IN THE NAVY

Americans came to love the statue; it grew to be a national symbol of freedom, liberty, and justice. The statue even appeared on U.S. government posters and in advertising campaigns. Many people thought of her as the nation's female equivalent to Uncle Sam. (Uncle Sam is a fictional male character with a white goatee and a star-spangled suit often used to symbolize the United States government.) In 1924 President Calvin Coolidge declared the statue a national monument. By then, many Americans felt that the statue was a national treasure.

In 1903 a small but important addition was made to the Statue of Liberty. This addition was a bronze plaque with a poem inscribed on it. The poem,

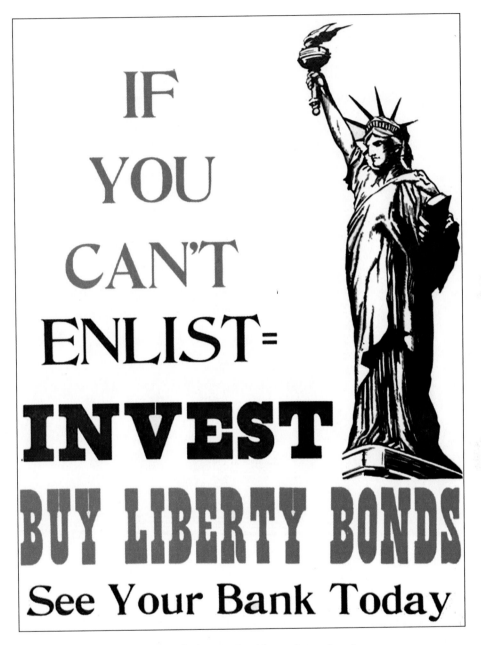

Because the statue inspires feelings of pride and passion in so many Americans, it has been used successfully in advertising campaigns throughout the years. The posters shown here and at left were created during World War I to encourage Americans to enlist in the Navy and to buy Liberty Bonds.

THE NEW COLOSSUS.

NOT LIKE THE BRAZEN GIANT OF GREEK FAME,
WITH CONQUERING LIMBS ASTRIDE FROM LAND TO LAND;
HERE AT OUR SEA-WASHED, SUNSET GATES SHALL STAND
A MIGHTY WOMAN WITH A TORCH, WHOSE FLAME
IS THE IMPRISONED LIGHTNING, AND HER NAME
MOTHER OF EXILES. FROM HER BEACON-HAND
GLOWS WORLD-WIDE WELCOME; HER MILD EYES COMMAND
THE AIR-BRIDGED HARBOR THAT TWIN CITIES FRAME.
"KEEP ANCIENT LANDS, YOUR STORIED POMP!"
          CRIES SHE
WITH SILENT LIPS. "GIVE ME YOUR TIRED, YOUR
          POOR,
YOUR HUDDLED MASSES YEARNING TO BREATHE FREE,
THE WRETCHED REFUSE OF YOUR TEEMING SHORE.
SEND THESE, THE HOMELESS, TEMPEST-TOST TO ME,
I LIFT MY LAMP BESIDE THE GOLDEN DOOR!"

―――――

THIS TABLET, WITH HER SONNET TO THE BARTHOLDI STATUE
OF LIBERTY ENGRAVED UPON IT, IS PLACED UPON THESE WALLS
IN LOVING MEMORY OF
EMMA LAZARUS
BORN IN NEW YORK CITY, JULY 22ᴰ, 1849
DIED NOVEMBER 19ᵀᴴ, 1887.

The poem written on this bronze plaque welcomes immigrants to America.

called "The New Colossus" or "Mother of Exiles," was written by Emma Lazarus, an established poet who was moved by the plight of immigrants. The poem serves as a welcoming message from the Statue of Liberty to people coming to the United States from throughout the world. At the time it

* * * *

was written, most immigrants arrived in the United States through New York Harbor. Therefore, the Statue of Liberty was one of the first things they saw. It reads:

Not like the brazen giant of Greek fame,
With conquering limbs astride from land to land;
Here at our sea-washed, sunset gates shall stand
A mighty woman with a torch, whose flame
Is the imprisoned lightning, and her name
Mother of Exiles. From her beacon-hand
Glows world-wide welcome; her mild
    eyes command
The air-bridge harbor that twin
    cities frame.
"Keep ancient lands, your
    storied pomp!" cries she
With silent lips. "Give me
    your tired, your poor,
Your huddled masses
    yearning to breathe free,
The wretched refuse of
    your teeming shore,
Send these, the homeless,
    tempest-tost to me,
I lift my lamp beside the
golden door!"

Emma Lazarus originally wrote "The New Colossus" in 1883 for an auction to raise money for the statue's pedestal.

The immigrants who came to America were again remembered in 1936, when a fiftieth anniversary

177

celebration of the unveiling of the Statue of Liberty was held. At the ceremony President Franklin D. Roosevelt said:

> Millions of men and women… adopted this homeland because in this land they found a home in which the things they desired most could be theirs—freedom of opportunity, freedom of thought, freedom to worship God. Here they found life because here there was freedom to live. It is the memory of all these eager, seeking millions that makes this one of America's places of great romance… It is fitting therefore that this should be a service of rededication to the liberty and the peace which this statue symbolizes. Liberty and peace are living things. In each generation—if they are to be maintained—they must be guarded and vitalized anew.

In keeping with that sentiment, steps have been taken to properly maintain the statue. By the 1980s

Once the gateway for more than twelve million immigrants entering the United States, Ellis Island now serves as a museum, telling the story of all those who passed through its doors.

ELLIS ISLAND

Ellis Island lies north of the Statue of Liberty. More than 12 million immigrants passed through the immigration center there when they came to America in search of a better life. Due to its historical importance, Ellis Island was declared part of the Statue of Liberty National Monument in 1965.

In the 1980s, the statue underwent a facelift in preparation for her centennial birthday celebration in July 1986.

time and weather had taken its toll on the monument, and some repairs needed to be done. Money was collected through donations for a multimillion-dollar **restoration** project that took about two years to complete.

All the repairs were completed for the statue's hundredth birthday. On July 4, 1986, the Statue of Liberty was the centerpiece of a fabulous festival that lasted four days. Standing at the monument, President Ronald Reagan stated: "We are the keepers of the flame of liberty; we hold it high for the world to see." That night there was a light show over the harbor and a magnificent fireworks display lit up the sky. Television viewers around the world saw the statue in its full glory.

A second ceremony was held at the Statue of Liberty on October 28, 1986, to mark the one-hundred-year anniversary of the statue's original dedication. When the statue had first gone up in the United States, Bartholdi looked at the finished product with pleasure. He is quoted as saying, "The dream of my life is accomplished." If he were alive today, he'd be pleased to see how much his dream has come to mean to all Americans.

Fireworks burst around the Statue of Liberty during the spectacular celebration of a national monument.

Timeline: The Statue of

1865	1870	1871	1875	1876	1877	1878
 Professor Édouard-René de Laboulaye suggests the idea for a statue honoring liberty.	France declares war on Germany, and the Franco-Prussian War begins. Sculptor Frédéric-Auguste Bartholdi serves in the military.	Bartholdi goes to America to look for a site for the Statue of Liberty and win America's support for the project.	The Franco-American Union is formed.	The Statue of Liberty's arm and torch are displayed in Philadelphia and New York City.	 Congress approves Bedloe's Island as the site for the statue.	The Statue of Liberty's head is displayed at the Paris Universal Exposition of 1878.

Liberty

1880	1883	1884	1885	1886	1903	1924
Gustave Eiffel designs the framework for the Statue of Liberty.	Laboulaye dies before the statue's completion.	The finished statue is presented to the American people at a ceremony in Paris. It is displayed in France before being shipped to the United States.	The statue is dismantled and shipped to America.	The Statue of Liberty is assembled in the United States and dedicated in October.	The poem "The New Colossus" is inscribed on a plaque for the Statue of Liberty.	The Statue of Liberty is made a national monument.

1956	1965	1984	1986
The name of Bedloe's Island is changed to Liberty Island.	Ellis Island is made part of the Statue of Liberty National Monument.	Broad-scale repairs begin on the statue.	Lady Liberty is one hundred years old. The statue's centennial is celebrated on the Fourth of July.	On October 28, the one hundredth anniversary of the statue's original dedication is celebrated.

★ ★ ★ ★

CHAPTER 6

THE TOMB OF THE UNKNOWN SOLDIER

ROGER WACHTEL

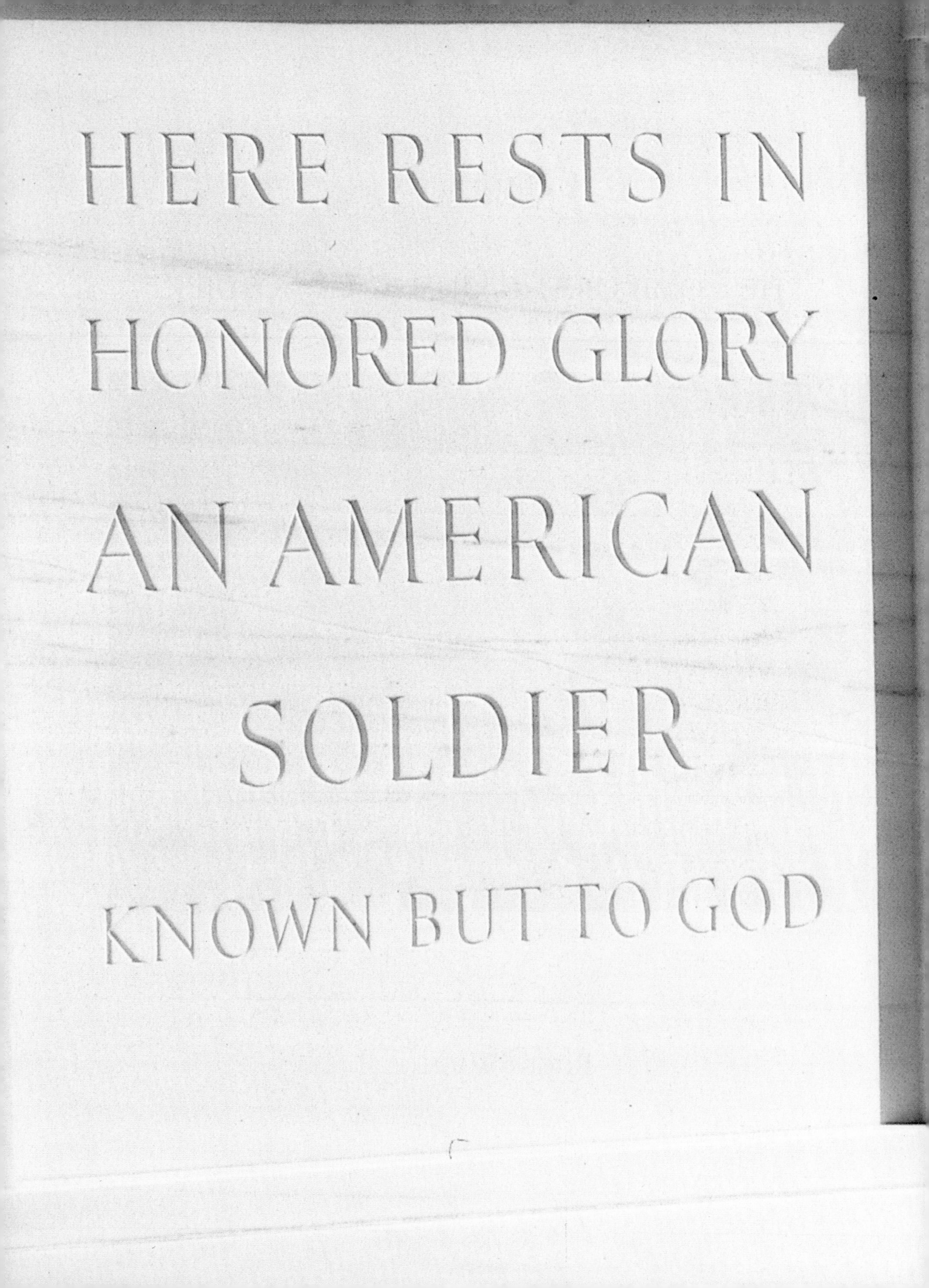

HERE RESTS IN
HONORED GLORY
AN AMERICAN
SOLDIER
KNOWN BUT TO GOD

In Arlington National Cemetery, on a hill overlooking Washington, D.C., is the most honored gravesite in America. While it is surrounded by the burial places of more than 200,000 men and women, many of them famous and highly decorated soldiers, it is the only one with a permanent military guard. Millions of people visit it each year, yet no one even knows who is buried there. As the inscription on the tomb says, "Here rests in honored glory an American Soldier known but to God."

Robert E. Lee came to own Arlington House when he married the great-granddaughter of George Washington, Mary Anna Custis. They lived there until 1861, though Lee was frequently away. On May 24, 1861, Union troops occupied the estate. Officers lived in the house while soldiers camped on the grounds.

The Tomb of the Unknown Soldier is found at Arlington National Cemetery, the most famous of many American military cemeteries. It is located just across the Potomac River from Washington, D.C. It was established there during the Civil War when General Montgomery Meigs decided to punish Confederate General Robert E. Lee by using his land for the burial of the mounting numbers of Union dead. After the war, the government paid the Lees for the land, but Meigs got his way. The 16,000 soldiers who were buried there guaranteed the Lees would never return.

★ ★ ★ ★

Although today one must meet certain qualifications to be buried at Arlington, it originally served during the Civil War as a site to bury fallen soldiers whose families were too poor to have their remains shipped home. This often took place without ceremony.

NATIONAL MILITARY CEMETERIES

There are many military cemeteries located in the United States. They are reserved for soldiers, sailors, airmen, and marines who have died in battle and for those who have served with distinction. Their funerals are performed with military honors and the graves are cared for by the U.S. government. Two of the most famous of these are in Arlington, Virginia, and Gettysburg, Pennsylvania. Abraham Lincoln dedicated the Gettysburg cemetery with the Gettysburg Address.

Civil War battles were often furious, and the armies moved on as soon as they were over. Often, old men and boys who were unfit for the army were paid to clean up the battlefields and bury the men. Unless the dead had some identification with them, the

The bloodiest one-day battle in American history took place on September 17, 1862, at Antietam, in northwest Maryland, in the second year of the U.S. Civil War. There were over 23,000 casualties on both sides. For days, the soldiers were left just as they fell.

gravediggers had no idea who they were. Since the battlefields were usually private property, the bodies could not remain there permanently. They had to be **disinterred** and moved. That led to more problems with identification.

In 1866, the unidentified remains of 2,111 soldiers from the battlefields around Washington, D.C., were disinterred and re-buried in a common grave under a stone monument near Arlington House. An inscription on the monument reads, "Beneath this stone

It normally took a week to bury all the dead after a battle during the Civil War. When soldiers buried their own, they had to do so quickly in order to move on to the next battle. This led to much confusion in identifying the deceased.

repose the bones of two thousand one hundred eleven unknown soldiers gathered after the war from the fields of Bull Run . . . Their remains could not be identified, but their names and deaths are recorded in the archives of their country, and its grateful citizens honor them as of their noble army of martyrs. May they rest in peace." They remain there today in the first tomb of unknown soldiers.

WHO CAN BE BURIED AT ARLINGTON?

Members of the military who die on active duty, those who retire from the military, and reservists with long terms of service are eligible for burial at Arlington. Those who have been highly decorated and anyone who has been held as a prisoner of war can also request burial there. There have been notable exceptions made, including personnel killed in the 2001 terrorist attack on the Pentagon and other notable citizens. The spouses of those buried at Arlington may elect to be buried there as well.

On September 12, 2002, a group funeral was held in honor of the victims of the attack on the Pentagon on September 11, 2001. The unidentified remains buried in Arlington Cemetery were in remembrance of all 184 victims.

On November 11, 1918, World War I officially ended. It was a war the scope of which the world had never seen. Then referred to as The Great War, it cost thousands of lives—136,516 from the United States alone. Other countries had their own devastating losses. While many of the dead were returned to their families for burial, many others were never identified. The unidentified men who had lost their lives far from home were most frequently buried in special cemeteries in Europe. Their families never had a chance to properly say goodbye, and the world's governments searched for a way to properly honor those who had given their lives for their countries.

The Battle of Verdun, in World War I, is considered one of the bloodiest in history, with a total of more than 700,000 killed, wounded, or missing on both sides. This blood was shed for a patch of land less than 8 square miles in area in northeast France.

The Arc de Triomphe was commissioned by Napoleon Bonaparte in 1806, but it was not completed until 1836. It was originally intended to honor France's unknown soldiers as well as its generals and major victories from the Revolutionary and Napoleonic periods.

France and England were the first to develop the idea of an unknown soldier. On November 11, 1920, both countries chose and buried one unidentified soldier to represent all those who could not be named. The French placed theirs beneath the Arc de Triomphe in Paris, located at the start of the Champs d'Elysses, Paris' grandest street. The English **interred** theirs in Westminster Abbey, where many of their

A horse-drawn caisson enters Arlington National Cemetery. The tradition of draping the flag over the deceased's casket was adopted from France, where it began during the Napoleonic Wars. In the United States, the flag is always draped so that the blue is at the head and falls over the left shoulder of the deceased.

MILITARY FUNERALS

Military personnel who are buried at Arlington receive military honors at their funerals. Their casket is pulled on a **caisson** or hearse, and draped with an American flag, which is removed and presented to family. A bugler plays "Taps" and a salute is given by a rifle firing team. The higher rank or more honored the serviceman is, the more involved the ceremony. Many funerals are performed at Arlington every day.

most famous artists and leaders are buried. The inscription on his tomb reads, "A British Warrior Who Fell in the Great War, 1914–1918 For King and Country." The Italians soon interred their own unknown, and many felt that the United States should as well. The original proposal for an American tomb was made by General William D. Connor,

195

commander of American forces in France. He had heard of the French project and was impressed with the idea. His superiors were not. He was turned down for two reasons. The first was the belief that eventually all the unidentified U.S. soldiers might be

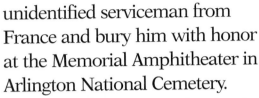

identified. The second was that the United States didn't have any place as appropriately impressive as the Europeans did. New York Congressman Hamilton Fish, Jr., decided there was such a place, and he introduced a resolution in December of 1920 to bring an unidentified serviceman from France and bury him with honor at the Memorial Amphitheater in Arlington National Cemetery.

The resolution passed to begin construction of a simple tomb that would serve as the base for a more appropriate monument at a later date. Congressman Fish hoped the burial would take place on Memorial Day in May of 1921. However, Secretary of War Newton Baker told the committee that the date was too soon. Only about 1,200 soldiers were still unidentified and all of those were still being investigated. If they buried a soldier too soon, he warned, he might later have to be **exhumed** when the government finally learned who he was.

Douaumont was part of the battlefield of Verdun in 1916. Over 300,000 unidentified French soldiers are buried at this national memorial to one of the most horrific battles of WWI. This photograph was taken in 1918.

American troops fire from trenches on the western front in World War I. The Germans were the first to use this method of warfare in an effort to hold onto occupied land in France and Belgium. When the Allies realized these fronts could not be penetrated, they, too, began to build trenches. It was in the trenches that some of the most horrific aspects of modern warfare were introduced—machine guns, gas attacks, and landmines.

A presidential election brought a new president and a new secretary of war, but still no unknown soldier. Congressman Fish again pushed for a ceremony to be held on Memorial Day 1921, but the committee finally settled on November 11, 1921, the third anniversary of the war's end. Plans began in earnest for both what form the ceremony would take and how the soldier would be chosen.

In September, the War Department began looking for soldiers buried in France who might represent all those who had been killed and buried anonymously during the war. A body was exhumed from each of the four American military cemeteries in France—Aisne-Maine, Meuse-Argonne, Somme, and St. Mihiel. Each of the four was examined to make sure that he had died of combat wounds and that there were no clues as to the soldier's identity. Then, the bodies were placed in identical caskets and shipping cases.

On October 23, at 3:00 in the afternoon, the four caskets were brought to Chaolons-sur-Marne. There was a large delegation of important officials from the United States military and government as well as France. The caskets were met by a French honor guard and French troops carried the shipping cases to the reception room in the city hall. The caskets were then removed, placed on top of the cases, and covered with American flags. At 10:00 P.M., six American **pallbearers** arrived and began to hold a constant vigil with the French guard.

Making sure the Unknown Soldier was truly unknown was very important. Early the next morning, October 24, 1921, an American officer

OVERSEAS MILITARY CEMETERIES

When soldiers, sailors, airmen, and marines die overseas, they are often returned home. Others are buried near where they died. More than 100,000 members of the United States military are buried in American cemeteries located overseas. Some of the best known are in France, near where the D-Day invasion took place, and in Hawaii, where many of the dead from Pearl Harbor and the Pacific Theater of World War II are buried.

On Memorial Day in 1930 at Arlington National Cemetery, Sergeant Edward S. Younger honored the fallen soldier whom he had designated nine years earlier as the symbol for all unknown soldiers. Younger was a highly decorated combat infantryman on duty in Germany when he first chose between the four caskets.

directed French and American troops to move the caskets. That way no one would have any way of even knowing which cemetery each had come from. The officer then designated Sergeant Edward S. Younger to choose the Unknown Soldier. Originally this was to have been done by an officer, but when American officials learned that the French had given this honor to an enlisted man, they decided to do the same.

The ranking French and American generals each made a short speech honoring the dead. Then Sergeant Younger took a **spray** of roses from a Frenchman who had lost two sons in the war. He walked around the coffins several times before placing the roses on the chosen casket. When later asked why he chose the one he did, he replied, "It was as though something had pulled me. A voice seemed to say to me, 'This is one of your pals.'" Younger then saluted the fallen soldier, as did the other officials. The pallbearers took the chosen soldier to another room. The other three were then removed to a cemetery near Paris, where they remain today.

Meanwhile, the body of the Unknown Soldier was placed in its special coffin and sealed before witnesses. It was draped with an American flag and the spray of roses. The utmost care had been taken to guarantee that this was indeed an unidentified soldier killed in battle. Equal care guaranteed that he was treated with honor and respect. It was indeed a perfectly executed and moving ceremony.

The Unknown Soldier was taken on a procession through the town the next day. Soldiers, firemen, policemen, and other dignitaries paid tribute as the honor guard took him to a special train for transport to Paris. The guard watched over him all night, and the next day more dignitaries paid him honor and presented him with memorial wreaths. The route to the ship that would transport him to the United States was lined with bands playing the American national anthem and military marches.

At the pier, the Unknown Soldier was presented with a French Medal of Honor. American Marines presented arms in respect, and the body bearers took him aboard the USS *Olympia*. Rear Admiral Lloyd

The body of the Unknown Soldier is carried from the USS Olympia at the Navy Yard while America's highest dignitaries of state, army, and navy stand at salute. General John J. Pershing and the Secretary of War, John Weeks, are among those in attendance.

Army Chief of Staff General John Joseph Pershing visited France in 1921, on behalf of President Warren G. Harding, to present the Congressional Medal of Honor to the French Unknown Soldier. Pershing had commanded the U.S. troops in Europe during World War I.

Chandler, commander, escorted the casket to the rear of the ship which had been decorated for the occasion. As *Olympia* left the dock, it was escorted by an American destroyer and eight French navy ships. *Olympia* received a 17-gun salute as it set sail for the United States.

The plans for honoring and burying the Unknown Soldier were just as elaborate, if not more so, as the ceremonies had been in France. On November 9, the *Olympia* sailed up the Potomac River into Washington, receiving military honors from posts along the way. When it docked, the most distinguished military leaders were on hand to

President Warren G. Harding places a wreath on the casket of the Unknown Soldier in the rotunda of the Capitol on November 9, 1921. Two days later he would give an emotional speech in honor of the Unknown Soldier and plea for an end to war.

receive the honored dead. Among them were John J. "Black Jack" Pershing, the highly decorated soldier and General of the Armies, as well as the Chief of Naval Operations and the Commandant of the Marine Corps. The Secretaries of War and the Navy attended, along with the 3rd Cavalry, whose job it would be to escort the soldier to the tomb.

As the casket was taken ashore, it was given the honors a full admiral would receive. A band played Chopin's *Funeral March* and the ship's guns began

The eternal flame that burns at the grave of former president John F. Kennedy was the idea of his widow, Jacqueline Kennedy, inspired by her visit to the memorial of the Unknown Soldier at the Arc de Triomphe in Paris, France, where a similar flame burned.

FAMOUS BURIALS AT ARLINGTON

There are many famous people buried at Arlington National Cemetery. President John F. Kennedy and his brother Robert, both of whom were assassinated, are there. Others include astronaut Gus Grissom, who was killed in a fire aboard *Apollo One*, famous generals Omar Bradley and Jack "Black" Pershing, and polar explorer Admiral Robert E. Byrd. Also in Arlington are boxer Joe Louis and Abner Doubleday, who is often credited with inventing baseball.

firing. As he left the ship, a marine bugler played a flourish and the band played the national anthem. The casket was placed on a caisson and the band played "Onward Christian Soldiers." The soldiers and dignitaries then joined in a procession toward the Capitol.

When the procession arrived at the Capitol, the Unknown Soldier was moved into the **rotunda**, where the public could pay its respects. First, however, even more dignitaries visited. This time they were led by President and Mrs. Warren G. Harding, Vice President Calvin Coolidge, the speaker of the House of Representatives, the Chief Justice of the Supreme Court and the Secretary of War, all of whom left flowers. The next day, when the public was allowed to pass by in respect, the crowds were greater than anyone had dreamed. The rotunda was supposed to close at 10:00 P.M., but lines were so long that they were kept open until midnight. By then, 90,000 men and women had passed by to honor the Unknown Soldier.

The bearers who took the Unknown Soldier to Arlington were all non-commissioned officers. Like everything else done that day, they were chosen so that the symbolism and ceremony of the day would pay due respect to those Americans who had lost their lives in battle. The procession included clergy, the president and vice president, all the military leadership in the country, members of Congress and the Supreme

The original funeral procession for the first Unknown Soldier commences from the steps of the U.S. Capitol, November 11, 1921. It would take over three hours for the procession to reach Arlington National Cemetery, where over 5,000 attendees would observe the ceremony from the Memorial Amphitheater.

Court, and officials from all over the United States. Also in the column was a special group of soldiers who had received the Medal of Honor.

The procession left the Capitol at 8:00 A.M. on November 11, 1921. As it did, an artillery battery began firing once every minute. They would continue to do so throughout the ceremonies, except for a two-minute silence at noon. The procession passed

* * * *

The Unknown Soldier is committed to his final resting place in Arlington National Cemetery. The bottom of the crypt had been lined with a layer of soil from France, where the deceased had first been buried.

through Washington toward the cemetery for more than three hours, finally arriving at the amphitheater at about 11:40.

The ceremony began in earnest after the moment of silence at noon. The assembled sang "America," and President Harding made an address paying tribute to the soldier and pleading for an end to war. He then placed a Distinguished Service Cross and Medal of Honor on the casket. Foreign dignitaries also

208

bestowed honors on the soldier, many of which had never been given to a soldier of a foreign nation before. Readings from the Bible and hymns followed. "Nearer My God to Thee" closed the ceremony.

The procession then moved to the tomb itself. The clergy read the burial service and Congressman Fish, the man who had initiated the legislation making way for the Tomb of the Unknown Soldier, placed a wreath on the casket. Plenty Coups, Chief of the Crow Nation representing Native Americans, placed his war bonnet on the tomb. The artillery battery fired three shots as the casket was lowered into the tomb, the bottom of which was covered with soil from France. A bugler played "Taps," and the battery fired a twenty-one-gun salute to honor the Unknown Soldier of World War I.

The World War I Unknown Soldier lay alone for years before the government decided to add more fallen men to the tomb. Meanwhile, changes were made to the tomb's exterior.

In 1932, a large **sarcophagus**, which had been called for but not funded in the original legislation, was added. The marble's engravings hold much symbolism: On the east side are three figures which represent the three allies from World War I. They also represent victory, valor, and peace. The peace figure has a palm branch to reward the devotion and sacrifice that, with courage, "make the cause of righteousness triumphant." The other sides each have

Family members are not allowed onboard military vessels for the burials at sea of a fallen member of the armed forces. However, the next of kin is quickly contacted with information about the ceremony. Here, the ceremony is performed in November 1943 for two sailors who were aboard an aircraft carrier torpedoed by a Japanese submarine.

THE MEDAL OF HONOR

The Medal of Honor is the United States' highest military decoration. It is awarded for soldiers who perform acts of bravery "above and beyond the call of duty." Frequently these acts put the recipients' life in danger, and many are given to soldiers who died saving others' lives. They are also awarded to U.S. Unknown Soldiers. The only Medals of Honor ever given to foreign soldiers were awarded to other countries' unknowns.

three inverted wreaths. The one facing the amphitheater bears the famous inscription, "Here rests in honored glory an American Soldier known but to God."

In 1956, President Dwight Eisenhower signed a bill to honor unknown soldiers from World War II and Korea just as they had been honored for World War I. He had been the commanding general of Allied troops in World War II, so it seemed appropriate that he would oversee these ceremonies. These soldiers were selected and honored much the same way as the

Sergeant Ned Lyle chooses the Korean Unknown Soldier in May 1958 in Hawaii. The Korean conflict ended on June 27, 1953, after 37 months of fighting and 3 million casualties.

World War I unknown had been. The official ceremonies occurred in 1958.

The World War II unknown was selected from soldiers exhumed from cemeteries in Europe and the Pacific. They were placed in identical caskets aboard the USS *Canberra*, and Navy Hospitalman 1st Class William Charette, the Navy's only active duty Medal of Honor recipient, chose one for interment at Arlington. The other was given a burial at sea with full honors.

Four Korean War unknowns were disinterred from a military cemetery in Hawaii. Army Master Sergeant Ned Lyle chose the soldier to be interred. Both the World War II and Korean caskets arrived in Washington on May 28, 1958, and lay in the rotunda until May 30. On that day, they were carried to Arlington National Cemetery on caissons just as their World War I comrade had been. There, President Eisenhower awarded them the Medal of Honor and they were interred on the plaza next to the sarcophagus.

In 1920, Secretary of War Newton Baker warned that choosing an unknown soldier too soon would be a mistake. He was afraid that after the unknown had been buried, army investigators would discover his identity and he would have to be exhumed. While it didn't happen then, it did 78 years later.

Advances in medicine and record keeping made finding an unknown soldier from the Vietnam War more difficult than it had been for the other wars.

Though Congress called for a search for a Vietnam unknown in 1973, it wasn't until 1984, some nine years after the official end of the war, that Sergeant Major and Medal of Honor recipient Alan Jay Kellogg, Jr., designated the Vietnam unknown.

President and Mrs. Ronald Reagan and many Vietnam veterans attended ceremonies in Arlington National Cemetery on Memorial Day, May 28, 1984. As tradition dictated, the president presided over the ceremonies and awarded the Medal of Honor to the Unknown Soldier and accepted the interment flag as honorary next of kin. At that point, however, the Vietnam unknown's experience became radically different than the others.

In 1994, a highly decorated Vietnam veteran named Ted Sampley began researching the circumstances around the time and place of death of the soldier whose remains were interred as the Vietnam unknown. He had been declared unknown because of the condition of his body and the fact that several kinds of aircraft had crashed in that area. There

Lieutenant Michael J. Blassie's fighter jet was shot down on May 11, 1972, by North Vietnamese anti-aircraft guns. Because the area was heavily controlled by enemy forces, no recovery attempts could be immediately launched. However, eyewitness accounts eventually led to Blassie's identification.

Jean Blassie poses with a photo of her son, Lieutenant Michael J. Blassie. For 26 years he was considered MIA before his remains were identified as the Vietnam unknown. Jean, who could not speak of her missing son for years, said, "In my heart I always knew he was gone, but there's always that doubt."

DNA TESTING

DNA (deoxyribonucleic acid) is a set of chemical strands that include genetic material. In short, it is the material that makes humans unique from one another. In recent years, scientists have been able to extract and "look" at DNA. Each person's DNA is different, so it can be used to identify people, even after death. Since humans share a large part of their DNA with their close relatives, DNA can be matched to find out if people are related.

seemed to be too many possibilities to make a credible guess of the man's identity as far as the military was concerned.

Sampley, however, used evidence that had been found nearby to determine that the body was that of a pilot of a single seat plane. That meant it was probably Lt. Michael J. Blassie. He published his information, which was reprinted by a national news organization. Blassie's family soon learned of the news and asked the Secretary of Defense to exhume the body and test its DNA to make a positive determination. In 1998, the body was positively identified as Lt. Blassie. He was returned to his family in St. Louis and then buried near his childhood home.

The question then was what to do with the Vietnam tomb. After much debate, the Department of Defense

A MEDAL REVOKED

The Medal of Honor is a very important honor, and usually there is an investigation to make sure the soldier who receives one performed an act of ultimate bravery. Since the unknowns were meant to represent all those who went unidentified, the government decided to award one to each of them. Since there was no evidence that Lt. Blassie had performed a Medal of Honor action, his Medal was revoked when he was positively identified.

The removal of the Vietnam unknown was an emotional moment for the guards at Arlington, who are honored to protect the unknowns year-round, throughout any weather. In the words of one sentinel, "They gave their identities and their lives for their country and ask for nothing in return."

determined that it was unlikely that another soldier would ever be truly unknown. Science has simply advanced so far that virtually any body can be identified. Instead, government officials decided to leave the tomb empty and dedicate a new inscription to honor those soldiers who are never found. They are declared "missing in action," and the uncertainty of that designation is very hard for loved ones left behind. For those soldiers and their families, the inscription now reads, "Honoring and Keeping Faith With America's Missing Servicemen." It was dedicated in 1999.

The U.S. Army Drill Team is one of the 3rd Infantry's specialty units. They perform numerous breathtaking drills to the delight of proud Americans, foreign dignitaries, and heads of state. To achieve perfection with their intricate maneuvers, they must practice constantly.

To most people who visit the Tomb of the Unknown Soldier, the most enduring image is the guards who watch it 24 hours a day. They stand in perfect military posture, ensuring that the men laid to rest there will never be disturbed. Visitors are often surprised to learn, then, that the tomb was completely unguarded from 1921 to 1925. In 1925, a civilian guard was hired to watch the tomb during the day, but it was left unattended at night. It wasn't until March 25, 1926, that a permanent armed guard was posted to the tomb "to prevent any desecration or disrespect." Now, only army personnel can be assigned to that duty. The army was so honored because it is the oldest of the service branches.

For several years, the duty moved from unit to unit, until 1946 when it was permanently assigned to the 3rd U.S. Infantry. The 3rd U.S. Infantry is an old and highly decorated unit of the U.S. Army established in 1784. It is referred to as the Old Guard. General Winfield Scott, impressed with the 3rd Infantry's fierce fighting, gave the unit the nickname during a victory parade during the Mexican War. People who have seen the Old Guard **sentinels** at the Tomb of the Unknowns have been just as impressed.

In addition to providing sentinels for the unknowns, the Old Guard performs other military ceremonies in and around Washington, D.C. That means more than 6,000 ceremonies a year, but the unit is by no means just a ceremonial one. It also provides military security to the nation's capital during any national emergency. In fact, members of the 3rd Infantry were instrumental in securing safety in Washington, D.C., on September 11, 2001, when the Pentagon was attacked by terrorists. It is based at Fort Myer, which is next to Arlington National Cemetery.

The Old Guard is known for two distinguishing characteristics. Every Old Guardsman wears a black and tan "buff strap" on his left shoulder. It is supposed to represent the knapsack strap that members of the 3rd Infantry wore in the 1800s. They also march in parades with fixed **bayonets** on their rifles. This honor commemorates a Mexican War battle when the 3rd routed Mexican troops with a bayonet charge. Only the Old Guard has this honor.

Guarding the Tomb of the Unknown Soldiers is extremely stressful, difficult duty. The soldiers who do so have to meet extremely high standards and maintain them for their entire period of service. It's not for everyone. In fact, it's not for most people—all the guards are volunteer. If they later find the duty is too difficult, they can transfer to other 3rd Infantry duty, no questions asked.

If a soldier wants to be a guard for the Tomb, or, sentinel, he must meet several requirements. These are so exacting that more than 80 percent of the applicants do not make it through the interview process. He must have a perfect military record and no criminal record. He must be in excellent physical condition and at least six feet tall. He must submit to

Among the various medals awarded for heroic service in the U.S. military is the Purple Heart (far left), established by General George Washington during the Revolutionary War.

intensive interviews with the sergeant of the guard, and officers of the 3rd Infantry. The interviews attempt to determine why he wants to be a guard and that his reasons support and respect the importance of that duty. The interviewers ascertain that the soldiers know how difficult the duty is. Many soldiers only

Mourners line the streets of Washington in late November 1963 to get a glimpse of the horse-drawn caisson carrying the body of President John F. Kennedy, who had been assassinated several days earlier. The horse being led behind the caisson bears an empty saddle. This is a tradition to show that the "warrior" will never ride again.

serve as sentinels for 18 months and few rarely serve over two years. As a former sentinel once said, "You have to be perfect."

Once a soldier is selected for guard duty, an intensive period of training begins. The months of training and practicing move each soldier toward the perfection every one of them is expected to achieve. Physical and mental fitness are stressed, and each is expected to become an

★ ★ ★ ★

expert on Arlington National Cemetery and the Tomb of the Unknown Soldier. They are regularly reviewed and tested, inspected and tested again. When they begin their period of duty, the reviews continue regularly to guarantee perfection. Guards are evaluated on uniform, posture, arm swing, heel clicks, timing, and walk, among other things. The intensity of these evaluations is one of the reasons guards serve such a short time.

All Sentinels of the Tomb wear a special insignia. It is a badge with a likeness of the Tomb surrounded by a laurel leaf. Underneath are the words, "Honor Guard." Anyone serving as sentinel for at least nine months is entitled to wear the badge permanently. The guards wear the Army Dress Blue uniforms while on duty. As they march back and forth protecting the Tomb, guards carry their rifles on the shoulder closest to the visitor, as a gesture of protect- ing the Tomb against any threat.

Even the guard's walk is steeped in symbolism. He crosses back and forth in front of the Tomb on a 63-foot rubber mat (placed there to prevent wear). He must cross in exactly 21 steps. At the end, he pauses 21 seconds, turns, pauses 21 more seconds, and retraces his 21 steps. Each time he stops, he performs a sharp click of his heels. Twenty-one is an honored number symbolic of the highest salute used in military ceremonies.

LAYING WREATHS AT THE TOMB OF THE UNKNOWNS

Many individuals and groups wish to lay a wreath at the Tomb of the Unknown Soldier to honor him and what the Tomb represents. To do so they must request and receive permission well in advance. They schedule their visit to the Tomb and are allowed, with the assistance of Tomb guards, to take part in a brief ceremony. About 2,000 wreaths are laid each year, including Veterans' and Memorial Day ceremonies, usually involving the president.

Members of the Kennedy family mourn at Robert F. Kennedy's funeral in Arlington National Cemetery on June 8, 1968. He had served as attorney general under his brother, President John F. Kennedy, before becoming a senator representing New York. He was slain on June 5, 1968, during his campaign for presidency.

Almost all guard activities are performed in silence. If someone attempts to enter the restricted area around the Tomb, for instance, the guard will stop and bring his rifle in front of him as a warning. If that fails, only then will he speak a warning.

Every hour, or half hour in the summer, the guard
is relieved and replaced in a short ceremony that
includes inspection of the guards' uniforms and
weapons. This is performed in almost total silence by
an officer of the guard. At night, the guard changes

The Changing of the Guard is one of the military's proudest traditions. The ceremony at the Tomb of the Unknown Soldier happens more frequently in the summertime to give visitors an opportunity to witness the event during daylight hours.

every two hours. While their watch is largely symbolic, occasionally people do stray into the restricted area and have to be warned off by the guard. In 1984, a disturbed civilian briefly took one of the sentinels hostage at gunpoint. In that instance, off duty guards disarmed him from behind and no one was injured.

The sentinels of the Tomb of the Unknown Soldier understand better than anyone the importance of their duty and the sacred nature of the place they protect. So that they never forget, one of their first obligations is to learn the Sentinels' Creed:

> *My dedication to this sacred duty is total and wholehearted.*
>
> *In the responsibility bestowed on me never will I falter.*
>
> *And with dignity and perseverance my standard will remain perfection.*
>
> *Through the years of diligence and praise and the discomfort of the elements,*
>
> *I will walk my tour in humble reverence to the best of my ability.*
>
> *It is he who commands the respect I protect.*
>
> *His bravery that made us so proud.*
>
> *Surrounded by well meaning crowds by day alone in the thoughtful peace of night,*
>
> *this soldier will in honored glory rest under my eternal vigilance.*

* * * *

Since the early years of Arlington National Cemetery, visitors have been overwhelmed by the sheer number of graves, arranged in military uniformity in honor of the country's war dead. Here, American flags adorn each grave in honor of Memorial Day, 2002.

When wars are fought, young men die. Many times they die alone and anonymously far from their homes. The Tomb of the Unknown Soldier recognizes this ultimate sacrifice on what is probably the most sacred ground in the United States. Whether it honors the soldiers who died and went unidentified, those who never came home, or the loved ones who miss their sons and daughters so terribly, the Tomb of the Unknown Soldier will ever remain one of our most important places of remembrance.

Timeline: The Tomb of

1778 | 1861 | 1864 | 1866 | 1919 | 1920

1778
John Parke Custis buys the land that will eventually become Arlington National Cemetery and Fort Myer Military Reservation.

1861
Union troops seize Arlington House.

1864
JUNE 15 General Montgomery Meigs proposes the Arlington House property as the site of the next military cemetery.

MAY 13 Private William Christman is the first soldier buried at what would become Arlington National Cemetery.

1866
The remains of 2,111 union soldiers are buried in a common grave as "unknown soldiers."

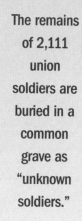

1919
OCTOBER 29 General William D. Connor proposes the burial of an unknown soldier, similar to the ones being proposed in France and England. His idea is rejected.

1920
DECEMBER 21 Congressman Hamilton Fish, Jr., introduces legislation calling for the tomb of an unknown soldier killed in action in France. The measure is approved the following March.

the Unknown Soldier

1921

OCTOBER 24
Sergeant Edward S. Younger selects a soldier from four exhumed from American military cemeteries in France, to serve as the Unknown Soldier.

NOVEMBER 11
The Unknown Soldier is interred in official ceremonies at Arlington National Cemetery.

1932

A large sarcophagus is placed on the Tomb of the Unknown Soldier, completing the project called for in the original 1920 legislation.

1958

MAY 30
Unknown soldiers from World War II and Korean conflict are laid to rest on the plaza next to the World War I soldier.

1984

MAY 28
An unknown soldier from the Vietnam War is laid to rest with his comrades from previous wars.

1998

After investigation, the Vietnam unknown is exhumed and positively identified as Lt. Michael Blassie. His remains are returned to his family for interment near his home.

1999

A new inscription honoring missing servicemen is dedicated on what was the Vietnam Unknown Tomb. Decision is to leave the Tomb permanently and symbolically empty.

★ ★ ★ ★

CHAPTER 7

THE VIETNAM MEMORIAL

SARAH DE CAPUA

JOHN M DONOHUE · JAMES C DURHAM Jr · JAMES R E
CHARLES M THOMPSON · RUSSELL J HEATH · BRADY V
H W KUCHCINSKI · LOWELL E LUNZMANN · JOHN M
AM J MOORE · CLYDE E MORGAN · RANDALL A THOM
LIAM J OSKILANEC · NORMAN W PARTRIDGE · TONY
JOSEPH F ROBLE · JOSE MANUEL RUIZ · ALFRED V SCH
EL R SUMMERFIELD · DONALD E GLIME · DALE A MOR
NNY BEE WILLIAMS · ARNOLD B WIMBERLY · MICHAE
· SAMUEL F BRYANT · ROBERT A BURKE · RICHARD A
EWAYNE CORBITT · EDGAR F DAVIS · STEVEN J DAWSO
· DAVID EISENBRAUN · RANDALL L FARLOW · BRUC
NLEY · WILLIE C HARDY · RAY A HAYES · TRISTAN W HA
HAEL W ISSENMANN · G B JACKSON Jr · GARY F JOHN
GE LEE Jr · LIONEL MALDONADO-TORRES · JERRY LEE
E MONISMITH · GREGORY MUNDELL · FRANK J M
PARKE · RONALD J POINTER · DOMINICK POLLAS
PAUL M PRESSER · THOMAS R RANGE Jr · JAMES P RA
· WILLIAM A RIDENOUR · RONALD L RONDO · ALBER
GE D SHANNON · ALBERT W SIRMANS Jr · GEORGE A Y
WARREN A SMITH · DARNELL J SONGNE · BILLIE G STI
ELESKI · RONALD W ZYDEL · LARRY H ALLEN · MICHA
ALD L BROWN · GARY L BROWNING · WILLIAM E BRU
FORD F DASHNER · STEVEN W DECKER · JOHN F DOW
ARLES L FREEMAN · JAMES O FRYMAN · JOE A GALVEZ
AY · RALPH L GREEN · WAYNE A HAYS · ROBERT L JANO
RISTOPHER D LUCCI · GILBERT M MAESTAS · JAMES R
M D ROBINSON Jr · JOSEPH SAROCAM · ALFRED M SO
MON · GARY E STRAKER · ISAAC TAGGART

Dale R. Buis. Rafael Cruz. Leon A. Hunt. Richard Vande Geer. These are just a few of the more than 58,000 names carved on the Vietnam Veterans Memorial. Located in Constitution Gardens on the Mall in Washington, D.C., the memorial is most often called simply the Wall. Since its dedication on November 13, 1982, it has become the most visited **monument** in the nation's capital. A monument is a statue, building, or other work that is meant to remind people of an event or a person. Visitors from all over the world make the Wall one of their first stops in Washington, D.C. There they view the Wall and the two statues that complete the memorial. No matter where they come from, people who visit the Wall are struck by the list of names that goes on and on. The names are those of U.S. service people who were killed or listed as missing during the Vietnam War (1959–1975). The memorial helps people to remember those who lost their lives. It exists to honor the men and women who served their country.

Prior to the 1950s, many Americans had never heard of Vietnam. Before long, the country came to hold an important place in the history of the United States.

Vietnam is a long, narrow country located in Southeast Asia. It borders the nations of China, Laos, and Cambodia. Beginning in the 1880s, Vietnam was a French **colony**, meaning it was a territory controlled by France. In 1946, unhappy Vietnamese who no

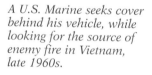

A U.S. Marine seeks cover behind his vehicle, while looking for the source of enemy fire in Vietnam, late 1960s.

The suburb of Haiphong in North Vietnam lies in ruins after U.S. bombing in 1969. Despite the military might of the United States, the North Vietnamese and Vietcong were unwavering in their loyalty and commitment to the cause of a united Vietnam.

longer wanted to be under French control started a rebellion, or armed fight against the government. The rebellion was led by a man named Ho Chi Minh, who was a **Communist**. Communism, in theory, is a system of government that strives for a classless society by eliminating privately owned property and distributing all economic goods equally among people. Its ideals are the reverse of capitalism, which is the

HO CHI MINH

Ho Chi Minh was born in central Vietnam in 1890. When he was twenty-one years old, he left Vietnam to study in France. During this time, he began to follow communism. In 1941, Ho Chi Minh returned to Vietnam and founded a Communist group called the Viet Minh. The Viet Minh fought for Vietnamese independence from France. When the Viet Minh took control of North Vietnam, Ho Chi Minh was named president. He died in 1969. The Viet Minh went on to defeat the non-Communist forces, including the United States, in 1975. Today, the largest city in Vietnam is known as Ho Chi Minh City.

system of government of the United States. Ho Chi Minh and his **guerrilla** army successfully drove out the French, who surrendered, or gave up, in 1954. That same year, the country was divided into two separate nations. North Vietnam was controlled by Ho Chi Minh. It was Communist. South Vietnam was not Communist. The United States supported the non-Communist south.

Elections, processes of choosing leaders by voting, were to be held in 1956 to make Vietnam one country again. However, the leaders of the United States, especially President Dwight D. Eisenhower, were afraid that the Communists would take over all of Vietnam. The United States kept the elections from taking place. U.S. leaders believed if Vietnam became Communist, the governments of the surrounding countries in Southeast Asia could also fall to Communist rebellions. It was in the best interest of the United States to try to contain communism, especially in its standoff with the Soviet Union, which was the world's first and most powerful communist nation at the time. This period of tensions and the race to develop nuclear weapons was called the Cold War. The idea of one country falling to communism causing other countries to do the same was known as the domino theory. As a **democracy**, or country in which government leaders are elected by the people, the United

States opposed communism because it limits people's freedom. The domino theory was the basis for the U.S. government's response to the Communist threat.

This photo shows damage resulting from the U.S. bombing of the ancient city of Hue in response to the Tet Offensive. "It became necessary to destroy it in order to save it," was what one U.S. officer said about the destruction in South Vietnam caused by such U.S. efforts.

WOULD VIETNAM BECOME THE NEXT KOREA?

The Korean Peninsula had been divided between the United States and the Soviet Union at the 38th parallel at the start of the Cold War. In 1950, after the last of the U.S. troops had left the newly established Republic of South Korea, Communist North Korea invaded in an attempt to force reunification. The United States then entered and fought against the North. At the beginning of the United States' involvement in Vietnam, many supporters compared it to the Korean Conflict, in which communism had been contained. However, with the Communist movement happening inside South Vietnam, it proved to be a very different war.

As elsewhere in Vietnam, one of the complications facing U.S. forces in Hue was the ability of the enemy to blend in with the civilian population. Here, U.S. soldiers go door-to-door evacuating civilians.

Rebels, people who oppose and fight against a government or ruler, in South Vietnam were called Vietcong. They fought against the South Vietnamese government. The Vietcong were supported by North Vietnam. Their goal was to help the Communist forces defeat the government of South Vietnam so the entire nation would be Communist.

As the Vietcong grew stronger, the United States acted. President John F. Kennedy sent 17,000 U.S. troops to South Vietnam between 1962 and 1963. They were sent to help train the army of South Vietnam.

In 1964, it was reported that the North Vietnamese attacked two U.S. ships called destroyers that were off the coast of Vietnam in the Gulf of Tonkin. However, it was later found that President Lyndon B. Johnson manufactured this incident in order to gain the authority he needed to attack North Vietnam. The U.S. **Congress** voted 98–2 to allow President Johnson to take any action necessary to fight the North Vietnamese in what was called the Gulf of Tonkin resolution. Between 1962 and 1975, when the war ended, more than 540,000 American soldiers were sent to Vietnam. Of those, more than 58,000 did not return alive.

As the war in Vietnam dragged on, some Americans began to question U.S. involvement in it. They believed the United States should not be fighting a war in Asia. Moreover, some Americans resented that so many young men, only eighteen to nineteen years of age, were being drafted into the war and killed because

This photo shows a demonstration on the Washington Mall against the Vietnam War. These protests increased in size and frequency following the Tet Offensive.

THIRTEEN YEARS

The Vietnam War, in which the United States was involved for thirteen years, was the longest war in U.S. history.

the United States did not want all of Vietnam to become Communist.

As more Americans shared this belief, the people of the United States became divided over the war. Millions of Americans believed it was important to support non-Communist South Vietnam. They agreed with the U.S. government position to keep communism from spreading in Southeast Asia. Americans began to argue with each other over what was best for the United States. U.S. military leaders believed the war could be won and asked for more troops to be sent to Vietnam. Many Americans who read newspaper stories and watched television programs of the soldiers fighting and dying, however, thought differently. They believed the war could not be won by the non-Communists. They wanted the United States to get out of Vietnam. One famous proposal was just to declare victory and then leave.

A wounded Marine is assisted by his fellow soldiers in Hue during Tet. The Tet Offensive marked a turning point of the war, as Americans realized that the optimistic reports of U.S. success in Vietnam had been exaggerated in order to win public approval for the continuing war effort.

By the late 1960s, throughout the United States, protests against the war got louder. Protestors gathered in parks, on street corners, and in other public places to **demonstrate**, or join together in protest, against the war. They shouted against the U.S. government and sang

U.S. Marines and Navy corpsmen tend to the wounded in the South Vietnamese city of Hue during the Tet Offensive in early 1968. U.S. forces were surprised by the attack, which coincided with Tet, the Vietnamese festival marking the lunar New Year.

THE DRAFT

The draft is the government selection of men to serve as soldiers. Its official name is the selective service. When young men reach the age of eighteen, they are required to register, or sign up, for the draft. During the Vietnam War, when the U.S. government sent notices to those who were required to report for military duty, many refused to do so. Burning their draft notices was a way to show government leaders that they refused to participate in the war.

A young man burns his draft notice. By 1969, the method for choosing young men to serve in the military was a lottery based on the potential draftee's birthday. Many of those drafted were likely to be assigned to combat duty in Vietnam.

peace songs. They burned American flags, and young men their draft notices. Many times, the protests turned violent.

It was a difficult and confusing time in the United States. Americans were left unhappy and disappointed in their government.

243

President Richard Nixon uses a television broadcast to explain the expansion of American involvement in the Vietnam War: "If, when the chips are down, the world's most powerful nation, the United States of America, acts like a pitiful, helpless giant, the forces of totalitarianism and anarchy will threaten free nations and free institutions throughout the world."

In 1973, while Richard Nixon was U.S. president, a cease-fire agreement was signed. A cease-fire is an arrangement to end fighting. Most U.S. forces returned home. In April 1975, the Army of North Vietnam ignored the cease-fire and invaded South Vietnam. The South Vietnamese army was quickly defeated. The few remaining U.S. military forces barely escaped being captured by the North Vietnamese. The Communist North Vietnamese had taken over the country. The war was over.

* * * *

The United States had lost a war for the first time in its history. Many Americans no longer had confidence in the government. They questioned the United States' involvement in Vietnam in the first place. Many thought it would have been just as disastrous if the United States had won.

Returning home to the United States was difficult for Vietnam **veterans**, people who serve in the armed forces, especially during a war. Veterans of earlier wars, particularly World War II (1939–1945), were welcomed home as heroes. Parades were held in their honor

THE SOCIALIST REPUBLIC OF VIETNAM

Today, Vietnam is still a Communist country. Its official name is the Socialist Republic of Vietnam. Many of its government leaders are the rebels who fought against French then U.S. occupation. More than half of its population of 78 million was born after 1975. This younger generation embraces many American products and trends. Though the older generation is still cautious and distrusting of the United States, to many young Vietnamese the war is "ancient history."

U.S. soldiers in uniform march down Fifth Avenue in New York City during a World War II victory parade. There was no such celebration for those who returned from Vietnam.

A homeless veteran on the streets of San Francisco, California. The treatment of returning veterans by many ordinary Americans made it difficult for those who fought in Vietnam to reenter society successfully. As a result, many suffered from unemployment and homelessness.

and government leaders praised them. Families, friends, and even strangers thanked them for serving the country. But this did not happen for the men who returned from Vietnam. Americans were tired of the long war. Many questioned the way the war was fought. They were appalled by the atrocities against Vietnamese civilians. An estimated 3 million civilians died during the Vietnam War. Stories of soldiers' drug abuse, including the use of heroin, had made it back to the United States. When the veterans returned, some were met with **hostility** from people they did not know. Veterans were even spat upon. These feelings were hard for the veterans to accept. After all, by serving in Vietnam they had simply done what their government had ordered of them. Their treatment by many ordinary Americans was unfair and disrespectful. It seemed that everyone in the country—citizens and veterans alike—just wanted to forget about the war.

Jan Scruggs, from Bowie, Maryland, was nineteen years old in 1969 when he decided to join the U.S. Army. He served for more than a year and was wounded. After Scruggs returned home to the United States, he went to college. That is when he first thought about a Vietnam veterans memorial. He believed it was important for Americans to remember the war. He thought a memorial to the men and women who served and died would help the people of the country get over their bad feelings about losing the war.

Jan Scruggs, pictured here, recounted this memory years later about his time in Vietnam: "January 21, 1970, was a typical morning in Vietnam for me. I was serving in Xuan Loc, a town in South Vietnam, with the U.S. Army's 199th Light Infantry Brigade. I had just cleaned an 81-mm mortar and was having coffee. Suddenly there was a deafening explosion. Smoke began billowing about 200 yards away. I ran at full speed and was first on the scene of the disaster. My fellow infantrymen—my friends—were all dead. I was 19 years old, and many of them were no older."

Many Vietnam veterans in the United States were having trouble getting their lives back to normal after their experiences in the war. They had seen so much death and destruction. They could not forget the horrors of battle. Some wondered why they survived the war, but their friends had been killed. Many had nightmares and flashbacks, sudden memories of events that were forgotten. There was not much support or compassion from the American public for these veterans and their troubles. Veterans believed there was no one to help them solve their problems. Many became bitter and regretted serving their country. Scruggs hoped that a memorial would help to heal these veterans' broken spirits.

A paratrooper from the 101st Airborne guides a medical evacuation helicopter through the jungle to pick up casualties near Hue in April 1968.

A U.S. marine warns his comrades to keep down as he fires a grenade launcher at North Vietnamese positions. The date is April 19, 1968; he is advancing in order to retrieve the bodies of comrades killed one week earlier.

By 1979, Scruggs was giving much of his time and energy to seeing his dream of a Vietnam veterans memorial become real. He decided that the best kind of memorial would be one that listed the name of every man and woman killed in Vietnam. He told people about his idea. They said it would not work. They believed the country was not ready for a memorial. They thought there were still too many Americans who were angry that the United States had fought in the war. Scruggs did not allow those people to discourage him. He continued to share his idea with anyone who would listen. Eventually, he found people who believed his dream was possible.

With the help of fellow Vietnam veterans Robert Doubek and John Wheeler, Scruggs started the Vietnam Veterans Memorial Fund. This organization developed plans for the memorial. It was also set up to receive **contributions**, or money given to help a person or a project, from citizens and other organizations

For one week in April 1971, Vietnam veterans protested in Washington, D.C., camping out at the Mall and dumping their medals, dog tags, and insignias at the base of the statue of John Marshall, the first great chief justice of the U.S. Supreme Court.

A LITTLE AT A TIME

Much of the $7 million needed to build the memorial came from ordinary Americans. Their contributions came in amounts of $1, $5, $10, and $20 until enough money was raised to pay for the memorial. The rest of the money came from private sources, such as corporations and unions.

throughout the country. At first, however, progress was slow. After one month, the fund had received only $144.50 in contributions. People thought this was proof that no one wanted a Vietnam veterans memorial. Still, Scruggs was not discouraged. He, Doubek, and Wheeler continued to work hard and to ask for contributions. Eventually, over 275,000 Americans contributed a total of $7 million!

Before the memorial could be made, the U.S. **Congress** had to pass a bill giving permission for a memorial to be built in Washington, D.C. Both houses of Congress—the House of Representatives and the Senate—passed the bill unanimously, meaning everyone agreed that the memorial should be built. On July 1, 1980, President Jimmy Carter signed the bill into law. It said that the Vietnam Veterans Memorial would be built on the Mall near the Lincoln Memorial. The Mall is a grassy area lined with trees where people can walk and visit various monuments to important leaders and events in American history. Scruggs was thrilled that the memorial would be built on the Mall, one of the most popular areas of the nation's capital.

The law said a memorial could be built. It did not say what the memorial would look like. That decision was left to the Vietnam Veterans Memorial Fund. However, Scruggs and other leaders of the organization did not know how to design or build memorials.

Tribute is paid to the fallen soldiers of Vietnam on Veterans Day, November 11, 1986. The seemingly endless list of names on the reflective surface of the Wall always seems to bring visitors closer to the emotional magnitude of the horrors of war.

They only knew that they wanted the memorial to draw Americans together. Scruggs also continued to believe that the memorial should contain the name of every man and woman who was killed or listed as missing during the war. Still, they had no idea how this would be done.

Scruggs and the other leaders of the Vietnam Veterans Memorial Fund decided to hold a memorial design contest. The contest was open to all Americans. The winner would receive a $20,000 prize and the honor of having his or her design become a permanent part of American history on the Mall in Washington, D.C. There were four guidelines for the entrants to follow: the design should be thought-provoking, compatible with the landscape, include all names of the dead and missing or imprisoned, and not make a political statement about the war.

In October 1980, the Vietnam Veterans Memorial Fund announced the contest to the nation. **Architects** and **sculptors** from throughout the country were especially interested. Competitors were given three months to prepare their designs. By the end of the contest, 1,421 designs were submitted. A group of architects, sculptors, and designers was chosen as judges to pick the winner.

The judges spent one week studying all of the designs. On May 1, 1981, they chose Entry 1,026 as the winner. They called the design "the finest" of all

MANY DESIGNS, ONE WINNER

When the memorial designs were spread out for selection by the panel of judges, they filled a large hangar, a building where aircraft are usually kept.

Memorial design winner Maya Lin and Jan Scruggs attend a news conference on October 28, 1981, in Washington, D.C. Lin fought for the names on the panels to be listed in chronological rather than alphabetical order so that a visiting veteran could find his time of service within the panel. "It's like a thread of life," she said.

WHO IS MAYA LIN?

Maya Lin is an American whose parents came to the United States from China in the 1940s. Maya was born and raised in the town of Athens, Ohio. A proud American, she was deeply honored when her design was chosen for the Vietnam Veterans Memorial. Since then, she has designed houses and buildings; the Civil Rights Memorial in Montgomery, Alabama; an outdoor chapel in Huntingdon, Pennsylvania; and many other major works. Today, she is considered one of the best public artists in the United States.

Since its dedication in 1982, the Wall has been the most visited national memorial. More than 40 million people have paid tribute to those fallen in Vietnam. From this view, Maya Lin's vision of the memorial cutting into the earth is evident.

the entries and agreed that it would be an excellent addition to the Mall.

Most people expected the winner to be a well-known architect or sculptor. Everyone was surprised when the winner's name was announced: Maya Ying Lin. No one had ever heard of her. That is because she was not famous. At the time, she was a twenty-one-year-old student at Yale University in Connecticut. She was studying to become an architect. It was not until she won the Vietnam Veterans Memorial design competition that she became famous.

Maya had visited the future site of the memorial before she created her design. Never having experienced the death of a loved one, she wondered how to make her design contemplative about loss and able to help people heal. She later recalled, "[Death and loss] is a sharp pain that lessens with time, but can never quite heal over. . . . I had an impulse to cut open the earth. The grass would grow back but the cut would remain."

On November 13, 1982, the Vietnam Veterans Memorial was dedicated. A crowd of 150,000, mostly Vietnam veterans from all over the country, gathered at the memorial. Jan Scruggs made the announcement he had waited so long to say: "Ladies and gentlemen, the Vietnam Veterans Memorial is now dedicated." Emerging from the earth, the Vietnam Veterans Memorial is a wall shaped like a wide V, made up of two sides, the

Making a tracing of the name of a fallen serviceman is a way of bringing a piece of the Wall home, to memorialize the young man who did not return alive.

east wall and the west wall. Each wall is about 247 feet (75 meters) long. The walls meet at the memorial's highest point, which is 10 feet (3 m) high. The height of each wall gradually decreases to the ends, which are 8 inches (20 centimeters) high.

Each wall is made up of seventy black granite panels on which the names of 58,227 men and eight women are **inscribed**, or carved. They are listed by date of death or loss. Beside each name is a symbol. A diamond means the person was killed. A cross stands for anyone who was listed by the U.S. military as missing or imprisoned when the war ended. If a person returns alive, a circle will be inscribed around the cross. If the body of an individual is returned, a diamond will be inscribed over the cross.

The first casualties, or people who were killed, occurred in 1959. They are listed on the east wall's first panel. The list of names continues to the east wall's seventieth panel, which ends with May 1968. The names are carried over on the seventieth panel of the west wall. The list continues back to the first panel of the west wall, which is dated 1975. The memorial was designed this way so that the beginning and the end of the war meet in the middle.

For the groundbreaking of the memorial to have taken place, the Vietnam Veterans Memorial Fund had to compromise with many Vietnam veterans who rejected Lin's design. Though they had strongly supported the idea of a memorial, when they saw photographs of Lin's design, they had taken back their support. They called the memorial "unheroic" and "a black gash of shame." Others simply called it "ugly."

They thought the use of white marble would make a better-looking monument than black granite. They wanted the memorial to be built aboveground instead of buried in the earth. They

CORRECTING MISTAKES

Some names on the Wall were inscribed incorrectly. When this happened, the corrected name was inscribed again, either at the beginning or the end of the same line.

believed a memorial showing some of the heroism of servicemen and women would be a better way to honor them than a wall. Maya Lin had been disappointed that so many people did not like her design, but she did not change it. "I hope they will give it a chance," she said. *Three Servicemen* and the Vietnam Women's Memorial were added to appease these opponents.

Near the entrance to the memorial site is the lifelike statue called *Three Servicemen*. The 7-foot-high (2-m) bronze statue is the work of sculptor Frederick Hart. The statue's placement is almost directly

The unveiling of the Three Servicemen. The work is placed so the servicemen appear to be looking at the names on the Wall.

The woman pictured here weeps for those friends she knew while serving as a nurse during the Vietnam War. This photo was taken on Memorial Day, 2000.

across from the Wall. The three young servicemen carry guns, ammunition, and canteens. The statue was dedicated on November 11, 1984.

The final piece of the Vietnam Veterans Memorial was dedicated on November 11, 1993. The bronze statue, by sculptor Glenna Goodacre, honors the women of the U.S. Armed Forces who served in the war. The statue shows three women helping a wounded soldier. Surrounding the statue are

WOMEN ON THE WALL

The eight women whose names appear on the Wall are: Eleanor Grace Alexander, Pamela Dorothy Donovan, Carol Ann Elizabeth Drazba, Annie Ruth Graham, Elizabeth Ann Jones, Mary Therese Klinker, Sharon Ann Lane, and Hedwig Diane Orlowski.

This woman has come to the Wall to pay tribute to her father on Father's Day.
She is a member of an organization of people who lost a father in Vietnam.
A Vietnam veteran standing near her can be seen in the reflection on the Wall.

eight yellowwood trees. They symbolize the seven army nurses and one air force nurse who were killed in Vietnam. Their names can be found on the Wall. In all, about 11,500 women served in Vietnam during the war.

Visitors to the Wall are struck by the number of names and the losses they stand for. People who visit the Wall looking for a specific name have an easy way to find it. A grove of trees stands near the memorial. In this grove are five stands. Each contains a thick book that looks like the telephone directory of a large city. Each book lists the name of every person on the Wall in alphabetical order. Beside each name is the wall panel and line number on which the name can be found.

Once people find the names of those they are looking for, they can make a rubbing of the name. A rubbing is a kind of image, or picture. An information booth near the memorial has paper and pencils available to anyone who wants to make a rubbing. These rubbings are especially meaningful to friends and family members of those on the Wall. It gives them a chance to have a copy of a loved one's name as it appears on the Wall.

HOW TO MAKE A RUBBING

A rubbing is easy to make. Place a piece of paper over a surface that is engraved or has raised letters or images. Hold the paper steady and rub it with a lead or colored pencil, or a crayon. Be sure to hold the pencil or crayon at an angle and rub with the side of the point, not the tip. When you can clearly see the covered image on the paper, you are finished.

Sometimes people leave items along the base of the Wall. Flowers, flags, teddy bears, letters and cards, photos, and medals are among the many different kinds of offerings left at the Wall.

Since the Wall was first being constructed, people have been leaving items at it. In fact, a military service medal lies buried in the concrete beneath the Wall. It was left by the brother of a serviceman killed in Vietnam. The National Park Service oversees the memorial. At first, rangers in the National Park Service did not know what to do with the items. They knew the offerings were meaningful, however, so they did not want to throw them away. Over time, the number of offerings at the Wall grew. The Park Service decided that each item left at the Wall would be kept permanently, like items in a museum. The collection, which today numbers more than 35,000 items, is known as the Vietnam Veterans Memorial Collection. Every night, park rangers collect items left at the Wall during the day. They are taken to a storage building in nearby Lanham, Maryland.

What should people do if they cannot go to Washington, D.C., to see the Wall? The Wall can go to them!

In 1996, the Vietnam Veterans Memorial Fund introduced a **replica**, an exact copy, of the Wall. It is designed to travel to communities throughout the United States. The traveling exhibit is called *The Wall That Heals*. It is part of a program known as "Bringing the Wall Home." The program was created as a way

FLOWERS AND FLAGS

Only two kinds of items left at the Wall are not saved: flowers and American flags without messages written on them. Ribbons and messages on the flowers are removed and taken to the storage facility. The flags are donated to the Boy Scouts, Girl Scouts, and other patriotic organizations.

Some Vietnam veterans began a tradition of leaving their old combat boots at the Vietnam Memorial in memory of their fallen comrades.

for those named on the Wall to "visit" their hometowns and be among friends and family again. The traveling exhibit also helps veterans who have been unable or unwilling to visit the Wall in Washington,

A Vietnam veteran visits The Wall That Heals in Long Beach, California, in 2002. It was the first time the traveling Vietnam Veterans Memorial had appeared in Long Beach. The wall lists over 100 service people from the area who were killed in Vietnam.

D.C., to see it in the familiar surroundings of their own communities.

In addition to the replica, the Traveling Museum and Information Center includes exhibits and materials about the Vietnam War, the memorial, and the service people listed on the Wall.

ONE COMMUNITY'S EXPERIENCE

When *The Wall That Heals* was exhibited in Janesville, Wisconsin, in September 2000, 50,000 people came to view it. Community volunteers took turns reading aloud the names of the 58,220 service people on the Wall. The nonstop reading took fifty-one hours—more than two days—to complete.

In 1999, The Wall That Heals made its first international appearance in Ireland to honor the Irish-American casualties of Vietnam.

The Wall That Heals has visited more than one hundred towns and cities throughout the United States. In many communities, ceremonies are held for the family members of those on the Wall.

The exhibit's first international trip took place in April 1999. It was taken to Ireland to honor Irish-born casualties of the Vietnam War and the Irish-Americans who served in the armed forces.

No one who worked to make the Vietnam Veterans Memorial a reality thought it would become the most visited monument in Washington, D.C. It is more than a monument, however. It is a place where visitors gather to remember the men and women who served their country with honor in Vietnam. There they express gratitude to those who fought for freedom. It is a site of deep meaning and importance for

U.S. soldiers lead captured Vietcong guerrillas onto an army helicopter from a flooded rice paddy in South Vietnam.

A Vietnam veteran visits the Wall on the tenth anniversary of the end of the longest war in American history.

CHARLES J GIBILTERRA Jr · LAWRENCE F GREER · WAYNE D GROAT
DAVID F HEISER · DOUGLAS E HOFFMAN · HOMER W HOLLISTER
GE E JACKSON · RANDALL L JENKINS · CARL R KECK · ASA MARTIN Jr
· LARRY W NEILL · ARTHUR A CALLISTER · RAYMOND NITO RIVERA
I ROMERO · PAUL C RUDY · THEODORE M RUSH · RONALD SABIN
· JOHN J SENOR · KENNETH H SHELLEMAN · LEONARD D SMITH Jr
L A TRESSLER Jr · JAMES B WHITE · RAY M WILLIAMS · JERRY R DAVIS
N · ISIAH BARNES Jr · RONALD G BAUGHMAN · DONALD C BERRY
LO CASSIDY · THOMAS CLARK · OTIS J DARDEN · ALVIN J DERRICK
ANT · GORDON D GARDNER · GARY LEE GLEAR · DENNIS J GULLA
NSEN · LESLIE A JERSTAD · LESTER JOHNSON Jr · WILLIAM R LARKIN
· MICHAEL S MASSONE · WILLIAM H MILLER · RICKEY C C McCOY
MUSSEN · JOHN R REBITS · ROBERT E SHERLOCK · JAMES E SKIPPER
EMPLE · JOHN T WALLS · DENNIS R WHICKER · DAVID R AUGUSTUS
CHAEL A BARNES · ROBERT E BEAUMONT · BENJAMIN H BINEGAR Jr
H H BRUBAKER Jr · LEE E BURNOR · JIMMY O CALL · JAMES D CAMP
S · ANTHONY A BARBARINO · JOHN A DURHAM · ROBERT L EATON
J GILDOW · OTIS GREEN · ANDREW M HAGLAGE · ROBERT K HALL
II · DAVID HOWZE Jr · GREGORY J NICCOLI · ANTHONY A KOSTER
HL · ANTHONY L QUINN · HAROLD R RICHARDSON · JUAN RIVERA
NT · GERALD L THOMAS · HOUSTON F THOMAS · JAMES W TUCK Jr
WALKER · FRANKIE R WILLIAMS · RAY L GOOD · WILLIAM E BOEHM
BURKHART · JAMES L CLARK · LOUIS J CLEVER · JAMES V DORSEY Jr
O · BRUCE B BERNSTEIN · ALVIN GORDON Jr · GERALD J JOHNSON
· GARY R HALEY · ROBERT W HAMLIN · TIMOTHY M HARRINGTON
ARD · WILLIAM C JACKSON · GARY M JOHNSON
ER J KMIT · HOME DONADO-AGUILAR
SKEY · CLARENCE L NEUBAUER
N Jr · JOHN E NORDEL OLSON
YOR · RUSSELL E REINE RUIS Jr
· JOHN W SPAE GART Jr
· DANA L ZA RISTIANSEN
RRIS · MICH S M KEITH
CHTA · RAFA GDEN
RKER · DON OY
ON · TROY CHA
E · RICHA Jr G
BIBEY · G
H · ROBER
GARRETT
R JARVIS · G
LL · RUSSELL
TERSON

★ ★ ★ ★

the millions of visitors, most of whom never knew anyone whose name is on the Wall, who view it each year. Its permanent place in U.S. history ensures that one hundred years—and more—from now, 58,235 service people who left their families to fight a war and never came home will continue to be remembered.

These names are some of the 58,235 American dead or missing from the war in Vietnam. At its peak, over 200 servicemen a day were killed in action. The estimated number of Vietnamese dead, both military and civilians, is more than 2 million.

Timeline: The Vietnam

1959 1962 1964 1967 1973 1975 1979

1964 The North Vietnamese reportedly attack U.S. destroyers in the Gulf of Tonkin. More U.S. troops are sent to South Vietnam.

1967 U.S. protests against the war get louder as more Americans urge the U.S. government to admit defeat and pull all American troops out of Vietnam.

1973 North Vietnam and South Vietnam agree to a cease-fire.

1975 The Vietnam War ends with the Communist takeover of South Vietnam.

1959 The Vietnam War begins when Vietcong rebels fight to take over the South Vietnamese government.

1962 President Kennedy sends the first U.S. troops to South Vietnam.

1979 Jan Scruggs devotes much of his time and energy to the establishment of a Vietnam Veterans Memorial.

MY SON WAS KILLED! IN VIETNAM WHAT FOR? America

Memorial

1980

JULY
President Jimmy Carter signs the bill into law that will allow the building of a Vietnam Veterans Memorial.

. . . .

OCTOBER
The Vietnam Veterans Memorial Fund announces the design competition for the Vietnam Veterans Memorial.

1981

Twenty-one-year-old Maya Ying Lin wins the Vietnam Veterans Memorial design competition.

1982

The Vietnam Veterans Memorial is dedicated on November 13.

1984

The *Three Servicemen* statue is dedicated on November 11.

1991

The Friends of the Vietnam Veterans Memorial begins its annual Father's Day ceremony.

1993

The Vietnam Women's Memorial is dedicated on November 11.

1996

The Wall That Heals exhibit is introduced and begins touring the country.

★ ★ ★ ★

CHAPTER 8

THE WASHINGTON MONUMENT

ELAINE LANDAU

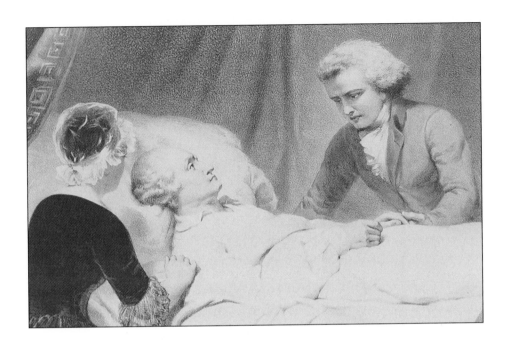

December 14, 1799, was a sad day in the young nation of the United States of America. Newspapers with thick black borders were spotted on nearly every street, announcing the dreaded news. It was the same news that caused women across the country to drape their dresses with black sashes and men to put on black armbands. These were symbols of mourning—a way for people to show their grief.

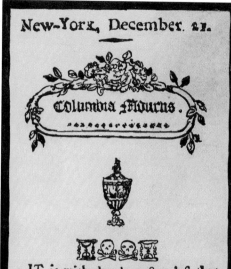

New-York, December. 21.

Columbia Mourns.

IT is with the deepest grief that we announce to the public the death of our most distinguished fellow-citizen Lieut. General George Washington. He died at Mount Vernon on Saturday evening, the 13th inst of an inflammatory affection of the throat, which put a period to his existence in 23 hours.

The grief which we suffer on this truly mournful occasion, would be in some degree alleviated, if we possessed abilities to do justice to the merits of this illustrious benefactor of mankind; but, conscious of our inferiority, we shrink from the sublimity of the subject.

Across the country, news articles sadly announced the death of George Washington.

That day, it seemed as if the whole nation was in mourning. George Washington, the nation's first president, was dead. Dying of a throat infection at his Mount Vernon estate in Virginia, his last words were, "'Tis well."

Most Americans would have agreed with him. Things had been going well for the new and growing country. The United States was a nation with a bright future. While serving in its highest office, Washington had done much to help set the country on the right course. Now the nation was left to deal with the loss of a much-loved statesman and leader.

Through the years, Washington's words and actions had shown Americans the meaning of **patriotism**. Some people doubted that the American Revolution would have been won without his leadership. Few of the colonists had military experience, and there was little money with which to buy weapons and ammunition to fight the British. Nevertheless, Washington took on the challenge of leading the colonists in battle. In 1775, he was appointed commander-in-chief of the raggedy, poorly trained fighting force known as the Continental army. After accepting the command, he modestly

Washington's strength and leadership during the American Revolution inspired the Continental army to victory. He is shown here directing the Battle of Princeton.

noted, "I beg it be remembered by every gentleman in this room, that . . . I do not think myself equal to the command I am honored with."

As it turned out, Washington was more than worthy of the command. Even with inexperienced soldiers and serious supply shortages, Washington led his men to victory.

★　★　★　★

When the fighting was over, some of his troops wanted him to be crowned the king of the United States. They respected and admired Washington and thought he would rule the United States wisely and fairly.

However, Washington scoffed at the idea. He had fought to help create a nation in which equality reigned, not kings and queens. Washington believed that Americans were capable of governing themselves. That was his dream for the country.

More than anyone else, George Washington was responsible for shaping the fundamental beliefs and values of our country.

While Washington had hoped to retire from public life after the war, he knew there was more work to be done. The United States needed to build a firm foundation. It was especially important that a constitution be put in place. The Articles of Confederation, the country's first constitution, left the government with few powers. It could not tax its citizens or control its borders. Washington knew that a weak government would have trouble protecting the nation in the future.

This oil painting, done by Howard Chandler Christy in 1940, depicts the signing of the Constitution. Washington is standing at far right.

So during the summer of 1787, a Constitutional Convention was held in Philadelphia, Pennsylvania. Its purpose was to create a constitution that would last through the years. Washington agreed to go to the Convention as a delegate, or representative, from Virginia. After arriving, the other delegates chose him to take charge of this historic meeting.

Washington was inaugurated, or sworn in, as president on April 30, 1789. He took the oath of office on the balcony of Federal Hall in New York.

The new Constitution required the nation to have a president. It was widely believed that Washington was the best man for the job. Electors from every state **unanimously** selected him. Washington accepted the offer. In 1789, he began to serve the first of two terms in office.

As president, Washington strengthened the military and the country's national banking system. He set the young nation on a course that would eventually lead it to become one of the world's most successful republics. In a republic, the people elect representatives to manage the government. That was Washington's hope for the United States, and he tried to mold the government in this way.

Washington turned down the offer to serve a third term as president. By then, he was about sixty years old and had already served the nation for a number of years. At that point, he longed to spend time at his beloved Mount Vernon home. In his farewell address, Washington urged all Americans "to properly estimate the immense value of your national Union." In saying that, he reminded his fellow citizens that their true strength was in their unity as a nation.

Washington was admired and respected when he died. Citizens of the young nation knew they had lost a great leader.

MOUNT VERNON

George Washington's favorite place was his Mount Vernon estate. Much of the estate's 8,000 acres (3,240 hectares) was used as farmland, but it also included a large house, groves of trees, and a lovely garden. Washington once said, "I can truly say I had rather be at home at Mount Vernon with a friend or two about me than to be attended at the seat of government by the officers of State and the representatives of every power in Europe."

Today, Mount Vernon is the most visited historic home in the United States, after the White House.

★　★　★　★

George Washington's death plunged the country into mourning. Washington's funeral took place in Virginia, and people around the country held services to honor his memory. Numerous poems and stories were written to praise him. For months following Washington's death, stores could not keep enough black armbands in stock to meet the demand. In death, Washington's reputation grew even greater. People began to think of him as a national hero.

Americans wanted to honor the man who had done so much for the country. Many thought that a monument would serve as a lasting **tribute** to him. A monument is a statue or building put up to honor a person or to remind people of an important event.

The idea of honoring Washington with a monument was not new. Even before his death, there was talk of erecting a statue of the man known as the "Father of His Country." In 1783, the Continental Congress (the early Congress made up of delegates from the colonies) proposed that a statue of Washington on his horse be built wherever the Congress's permanent home was to be established. The statue was never erected, in part because the government did not become firmly rooted in Washington, D.C., until 1800.

After that, other obstacles to the creation of the monument arose. When French engineer Pierre-Charles L'Enfant was hired to design the nation's capital, his plans included a

*Members of the
Continental Congress
discussed building a
statue of George
Washington as early
as 1783.*

Washington's statue was put on hold as the capital city was constructed.

A MUCH-HONORED STATESMAN

As time passed, George Washington would be honored many times in different ways. The nation's capital, as well as one of the states, was named after him. Numerous streets, counties, and universities across the country are named after the first president as well.

statue of Washington on a horse. Building the capital, however, took a great deal of money. At the time, there wasn't enough to go around. It was clear that the statue would have to wait until more money became available.

Washington's death brought on new pressures to act. The American people wanted their leaders to do something to honor him. A group of congressmen met ten days after Washington died to discuss how to proceed. At the time, Virginia representative

John Marshall suggested that a fancy tomb for Washington be built in the U.S. Capitol building in Washington, D.C. But Washington's family was not in favor of this idea. They had already buried him and refused to move his body. The proposal faced other problems, too. Any new project had to be put on hold because of the lack of funds.

Many years passed before work on creating a fitting **memorial** for George Washington finally began. In 1833, a year after the one hundredth anniversary of Washington's birth, an interested group of citizens got together to take over the task. The newly formed organization was known as the Washington National Monument Society.

After Washington's death, Virginia representative John Marshall proposed that a tomb be erected within the Capitol.

This certificate from the Washington National Monument Society was issued around 1849. It contains the printed signatures of various members of the society.

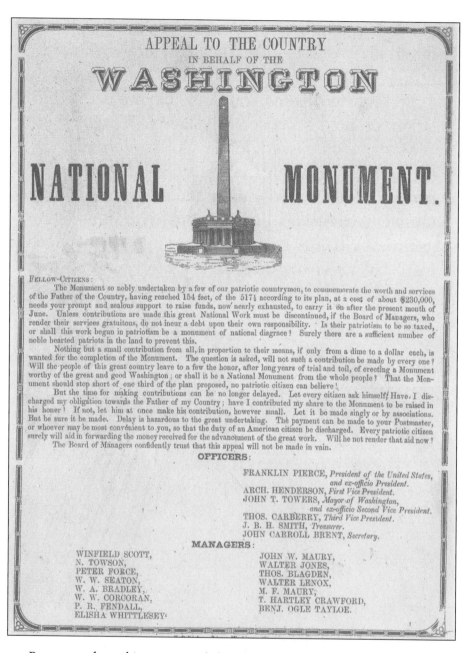

Posters such as this one appealed to the American public to raise funds for the construction of the monument.

★ ★ ★ ★

John Marshall headed this group. Although Marshall had wanted to build a tomb for Washington more than thirty years earlier, he and the other group members were open to new ideas.

As always, money was still a problem. Before any suggestions for a monument could be considered, the group needed to raise cash to pay for it. To spread the word about the monument, the society put notices in newspapers, journals, and bulletins. It sent representatives to churches, businesses, and various clubs and social organizations to ask people to help.

By 1836, the society had collected about $28,000. Its members were ready to start. At that point, no one knew what form the monument would take or who would design it. Nevertheless, the Society wanted the finished product to meet certain standards. These included being able to "blend stupendousness [tremendous size] with elegance" and "be of such magnitude and beauty as to be an object of pride to the American people." The monument was also to be 100 percent American. As the group put it, "Its [the monument's] material is intended to be wholly American, and be made of marble and granite brought from each state, that each state may participate in the glory of contributing material as well as funds to its construction."

In 1836, the Washington National Monument Society held a contest to find the best design for the monument. American artists and builders were invited to submit their ideas. The winner was an **architect** from South Carolina named Robert Mills.

Although Mills designed many public buildings, the Washington Monument would become his best-known structure.

Many people thought Mills was an excellent choice for the project. Mills was the first professionally trained architect born in the United States. Before entering the design contest, he had worked as an architect in such cities as Philadelphia, Baltimore, and Washington, D.C.

Mills had recently been appointed Architect of Public Buildings for Washington, D.C. He knew every street and waterway in the area. He had designed a number of important public structures in the capital city. Mills was also accustomed to working on tributes to George Washington. He'd already designed a monument—a statue of Washington on top of a tall column—in Baltimore, Maryland.

The monument Mills proposed for the capital was considerably grander than the one he designed for Baltimore. The centerpiece of his tribute to Washington was a 600-foot (183-meter) obelisk. An obelisk is a tapering four-sided pillar or column. The obelisk Mills wanted for the monument would have a nearly flat top. At the base of the obelisk, Mills planned to have a circular building designed to look like an ancient Greek temple. A statue of Washington in an ancient **chariot** drawn by six horses would rest on top of the building, which would be surrounded by a circle of columns called a colonnade.

In honor of Washington's leadership during the American Revolution, thirty other statues would be placed within the monument's colonnade.These would depict men who

*Robert Mills'
monument in
Baltimore was
completed in 1829.
It was the first major
monument to be
built in honor of
George Washington.*

This illustration shows Mills's early design for the Washington Monument.

fought bravely alongside him during the war. The finished product was to be a magnificent structure that would leave people in awe. It's likely that the proposed price tag for it would have had the same effect. The estimated cost for the monument was $1,250,000.

Work on the monument did not begin right away. Although the Washington National Monument Society had approved Mills's design, doubts about it soon came up. Some people felt the design was overly **complex**. Nearly everyone felt the cost was too high as well. Over the next few years, Mills submitted simpler versions of his original design to the society. At the same time, society members continued their fund-raising efforts. They knew that even a simpler design would cost far more than they had anticipated.

It wasn't until 1848 that work on a simpler monument could begin. By then, the Washington National Monument Society had collected $87,000. There were still questions about the monument's final form and design. For example, the group was not sure about the temple-style building and colonnade at the monument's base. So, construction began with the obelisk.

Members of the society hoped that the start of construction would make people become more interested in the project. Raising money for the structure with nothing more than a drawing had been difficult. The society thought that once people saw a real monument being built, they would want to contribute to its **funding**.

Raising money for monuments was difficult. Years earlier, during construction of the Washington Monument in Baltimore, lottery tickets were sold. The proceeds were used to build the monument.

★　★　★　★

Although many things about the monument were undecided, one thing was clear—its location. Congress had set aside 37 acres (15 ha) of free land for this purpose. Located near the White House, the site seemed ideal. It was also close to the Potomac River, which added to the monument's beauty. The river also provided an excellent means for shipping stones and other building materials to the construction site.

The Washington Monument would be close to the White House, shown here around 1850.

Blossoming cherry trees provide a colorful, scenic backdrop for the monument every spring.

THE NATIONAL MALL

Today, the Washington Monument is part of a nearly 2-mile (3-kilometer) stretch known as the National Mall. The Mall contains several monuments and memorials, as well as flower beds, pools, and fountains. The National Mall is also lined with two thousand American elm trees and three thousand cherry trees from Japan. Every spring, tourists come to the Mall to see the cherry trees blossom.

The society was pleased with the site. One of its members wrote, "[It] presents a beautiful view of the Potomac [River] . . . and is so elevated that the monument will be seen from all parts of the surrounding country." He also noted that "[It] would be in full view of Mount Vernon, where rests the ashes of the chief."

295

Digging at the monument's site began on April 18, 1848. Robert Mills was paid $500 per year to supervise the construction. Huge blocks of stone were needed just to get the monument's foundation started. Some of the blocks weighed as much as 8 tons (7.3 metric tons).

By summer, it was time to lay the structure's **cornerstone**. This event was planned for July 4, 1848, because George Washington himself was a great patriot. It was an event no one in the capital would soon forget. A crowd of more than twenty thousand people gathered for the ceremony. President James K. Polk was among the guests there that day, as were numerous Supreme Court justices and members of Congress. The crowd also included schoolchildren, firefighters, teachers, storeowners, barbers, clerks, and many other people.

The event was sponsored by the Freemasons, an international organization to which Washington had belonged. Many important Americans, including Benjamin Franklin, John Hancock, and Paul Revere, had also been Freemasons. The group was proud to play a role in honoring one of its most outstanding members. As someone remarked that day in a speech, "No more Washingtons shall come in our time . . . but his virtues are stamped on the heart of mankind."

It was a glorious day, and the monument seemed to be off to a terrific start. Anyone attending the ceremony might have thought this tall tribute to the nation's first president

GEN. GEO. WASHINGTON.

LAYING CORNER STONE, WASHINGTON MONUMENT.

Thousands of people gathered to celebrate the laying of the monument's cornerstone on July 4, 1848.

would be built in no time. Yet it didn't happen that way. Construction continued for the next six years, but then stopped. The Washington National Monument Society was out of money.

Construction on the monument continued steadily for about six years.

The society asked the government for money to help it complete the monument. Things began to look brighter when Congress agreed to set aside $200,000 for the work. Congress later took back the offer, however, just one night before the funds were delivered.

The trouble began after the society requested that every state contribute a stone for the monument's inner walls. This meant that the whole country would be represented within the monument. In addition to the states, foreign countries, religious organizations, business groups, American Indian tribes, and social clubs were encouraged to add stones as well. This practice got more people involved and helped spread the cost of the expensive stone blocks over many different groups.

Then trouble arose with the construction project. Ideally, no one was to be barred from helping with the construction of the monument. Some **prejudiced** people, however, wanted certain groups to be left out. Many of these individuals were members of a political party called the Know-Nothings. The Know-Nothings especially

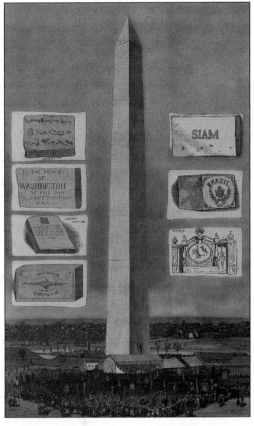

Stones from various organizations, as well as the states, were also used in the monument's construction.

DONATED STONES

The Washington Monument contains a total of 193 donated stones from various sources. These stones decorate the east and west interior walls of the monument. Alaska provided a magnificent jade stone that is worth several million dollars today.

THE KNOW-NOTHINGS

The Know-Nothing Party's official name was the American Party. While it claimed to represent "true Americans," it was a party whose beliefs were based on fear and prejudice. Because many of its activities were illegal, its members often had to act secretly. When asked about their plans, members were told to say that they "knew nothing." As a result, the party became commonly known as the Know-Nothing Party.

disliked **immigrants** and Catholics. They did not want these people to be involved in the monument's construction.

These feelings came to a head in 1854, when Pope Pius IX donated a block of marble to the monument. The pope is the head of the Catholic Church, and the Know-Nothings were not pleased with his gift. On March 6, 1854, the Know-Nothings stole the Pope's stone from the shed at the monument's construction site. They either destroyed it or threw it into the Potomac River.

The Know-Nothings wanted to take control of the monument's construction so that immigrants and Catholics would not be involved in building it. They launched an effort to take over the Washington National Monument Society. Through a fixed election held on February 21, 1855, the Know-Nothings seized the organization's leadership. They remained in power for several years.

This nighttime meeting of the Know-Nothings took place in City Hall Park in Manhattan in 1855.

During the war, the monument's grounds were used for more practical purposes. At first, the area became a drill field for Union soldiers. Later, cattle grazed there to supply beef for Union troops.

With the Know-Nothings in charge, all the Catholics and immigrants working at the site were fired. The society's fund-raising efforts were then directed only at "genuine" Americans. To the Know-Nothings, this meant white Protestants who had been born in the United States. The monument's progress and quality suffered during this time. Poor-quality marble was used in the construction, and many stones had to be replaced later. Unable to raise enough money to continue construction, the Know-Nothings began to lose control of the project. In 1858, they withdrew from the project altogether. The original society members took charge once again.

Yet work on the monument did not resume right away. When the Civil War broke out in 1861, people became preoccupied with the crisis at hand. The unfinished obelisk would remain at less than one-third of its original height for some time to come.

In 1866, President Andrew Johnson encouraged society members to continue work on the monument.

After the Civil War was over, interest in the monument stirred again. As President Andrew Johnson told members of the Washington National Monument Society in 1866, "Let us restore the Union and let us proceed with the monument as its symbol until it shall contain the pledge of all the states of the Union!" A decade later, in 1876—the one-hundredth anniversary of the signing of the Declaration of Independence—Americans were finally ready to act. Congress again promised to put aside $200,000 to help finish the structure. By then it had been under construction for more than twenty years.

Nevertheless, there were still some important questions to be answered before the project could go forward. The society had never settled on the final design for the monument. Some people thought completing the obelisk would be enough. Others argued that the obelisk was simply too "little . . . to be proud of." Before Robert Mills died in 1855, he stressed the importance of keeping the temple-styled building and colonnade. Otherwise, he warned that the monument was in danger of looking like "a stalk of asparagus."

On the one-hundredth anniversary of the signing of the Declaration of Independence, feelings of patriotism were high as people once again prepared to honor George Washington.

So, for a second time, the call went out for artists and architects to submit designs for the structure. Many new ideas came in. The society and Congress, which were then working together on the project, seriously considered five designs. The best of these was believed to have come from an American sculptor named William Wetmore Story. Story had worked and studied in Italy and was familiar with architectural styles abroad.

Story wanted to keep the monument's obelisk, but he had changes in mind for it. He hoped to surround the structure with an outer layer of marble. This new exterior was to be highly decorative. Story also wanted to change the monument's top. Instead of the nearly flat top that Mills had originally designed, Story wanted the structure to rise to a pyramid-shaped peak. The society liked Story's ideas. It said that his plan for the monument was "vastly superior in artistic taste and beauty" to the others that had been submitted.

However, as it turned out, parts of Story's proposed redesign involved some construction changes that the society was not willing to make. To use all his ideas, more than 40 feet (12 m) of the existing monument would have to be torn down and rebuilt. The fancy new exterior would also have added more weight to the monument than it could support.

In the end, it was determined that the obelisk built to honor George Washington would take a classically Egyptian form. It would be 555 feet (170 m) tall and **unadorned**, with the pyramid-shaped top that Story designed. At the time, there was wide public interest in the ancient ruins of Egypt. There, obelisks had been built to guard sacred temples from about 17 B.C. to A.D. 14. Many people admired the simple beauty of these structures.

An obelisk stands guard at the Temple of Amun in Egypt.

★ ★ ★ ★

Meanwhile, Congress ordered work on the obelisk to continue, and construction started again in 1879. The task of building the monument then fell to Lieutenant Colonel Thomas L. Casey of the United States Army Corps of Engineers. The newly redesigned monument would still be quite massive.

Lt. Colonel Thomas L. Casey directed construction of the monument from 1879 until its completion in 1884.

It was up to Casey to make sure that the foundation was both large and strong enough to support the structure.

This proved to be quite an undertaking. Casey had to create a second foundation that was two-and-a-half times larger than the first. Although the original foundation had been sound, the monument's new design required changes to its foundation. The new foundation went down 13.5 feet (4.1 m) deeper into the ground than the first foundation did. That meant a new cornerstone had to be laid because the first was then buried beneath the soil. The second cornerstone was laid on August 7, 1880, at the 150-foot (45.7-m) level, where building would resume. President Rutherford B. Hayes, along with several

The monument's foundation was strengthened to hold the additional weight of the new structure.

government officials, laid the monument's second cornerstone in a small, quiet ceremony.

Casey worked hard to complete the monument. He removed the poor-quality marble the Know-Nothings had

This photograph clearly shows the change in stone color halfway up the monument.

added to the structure. That reduced the obelisk to a height of about 150 feet (45.7 m). In ordering new marble stones, Casey tried to match the older ones exactly. He specified that these "must be white, strong, sound . . . and must in texture and color so conform to the marble now built in the monument as not to present any marked or striking contrast . . ." Unfortunately, this wasn't possible. Although Casey found the high-quality marble he wanted, he was not able to find the ideal color match. The monument had been started decades earlier, and matching stones were no longer available. Casey did his best, but a distinct color change can be seen above 150 feet (45.7 m) on the monument.

Completing the monument required a good deal of work. Slowly, Casey made headway. In time, he had the monument's inner iron framework in place. The framework helps hold the monument up. Produced by a Pennsylvania company, this structural piece was firmly secured to the inner stones. Meanwhile, the monument continued to grow taller. By August 1884, the Washington Monument stood 500 feet (152 m) tall.

Then, only the final phase of construction remained—the completion of the monument's top. On December 6, 1884, workers placed a 3,300-pound (1,498-kilogram) marble capstone (top stone) on the monument. The stone's point was removed and replaced with a solid **aluminum**, pyramid-shaped cap. It was the first time aluminum had been used in American architecture. The metal pyramid housed a lightning rod to protect the structure during storms. On the east side of the aluminum pyramid, the Latin phrase *laus deo* is inscribed. It means "praise be to God."

Two stonecutters work on the capstone of the Washington Monument.

On December 6, 1884, workers placed the capstone and a pyramid of cast aluminum on top of the monument, completing construction.

THE CROWN JEWEL

The aluminum cap on the Washington Monument is a great source of pride to the aluminum industry. Before the cap was selected for use on the monument, many people didn't even know what aluminum was. The fact that it was among the materials chosen for such an important structure served as a boost to the aluminum industry as a whole. Aluminum was a precious metal at the time, and the cap was treated like a jewel. It was displayed for the public at Tiffany & Co. jewelers in New York City before being placed on the structure.

February 21, 1885, was the proud day of the monument's formal dedication. It was a cold day, and there was snow on the ground, but that did not stop people from attending the ceremony. President Chester A. Arthur, who looked chilly even in his fur-lined coat, spoke fondly of the monument. Other officials addressed the audience as well. But perhaps the most meaningful words came from Lieutenant Colonel Thomas L. Casey. At the end of his speech, he turned to President Arthur and said, "For and in behalf of the joint commission for the completion of the Washington Monument, I deliver you this column." The monument that had taken thirty-six years to build was finally finished.

President Chester A. Arthur made a speech at the dedication ceremony.

As part of the celebration, there was a magnificent fireworks display in the nation's capital that night. One of the displays looked like George Washington on his horse. It lit up the sky as a glowing reminder of the outstanding patriot for whom the monument had been built.

The Washington Monument's story doesn't end there. Since its opening, visitors from around the world have come to see the Washington Monument. A short elevator ride has brought countless guests to the monument's observation

Photos of the monument reflected in the pool are a popular tourist item.

FACTS ABOUT THE WASHINGTON MONUMENT

- The total cost of the Washington Monument was $1,187,710.

- The Washington Monument is 555 feet, 5 -1/8 inches (170 m) tall. That's equal to the height of about thirty giraffes placed on top of one another.

- The Washington Monument weighs 90,854 tons (82,421 metric tons), about equal to the weight of seven male African elephants.

- There are 36,491 blocks of granite and marble in the monument.

- The thickness of the monument's walls at its base is 15 feet (4.5 m), but its walls taper to just 18 inches (45 centimeters) toward the top.

- 896 steps lead to the top of the monument, but these were permanently closed to the public in 1976. This was done to limit wear and tear on the monument.

- The Washington Monument was the tallest building on Earth until France's Eiffel Tower was built in 1889. The Eiffel Tower is 1,063 feet (324 m) tall, making it about 508 feet (155 m) taller than the Washington Monument.

- The fifty flags surrounding the Washington Monument's base represent the fifty states of the Union.

- The Washington Monument is the National Mall's oldest memorial to a president.

- The image of the Washington Monument is reflected in a pool called the Reflecting Pool. Located between the Washington Monument and the Lincoln Memorial, the pool holds 6,750,000 gallons (25,548,750 liters) of water.

313

From the top of the monument, visitors can get a good view of the surrounding area.

In 1999, scaffolding surrounded the monument as workers made repairs.

room at the 500-foot (152-m) level. From there, they can look out over all of Washington, D.C., and beyond.

Over the years, the effects of weathering and daily wear and tear caused by visitors took its toll on the towering structure. Experts warned that some of the exterior stones were beginning to chip, and pieces were starting to flake off. On rainy days, the structure had even begun to leak, damaging some of the interior stones.

Something had to be done before the situation got worse. Some **restoration** of the monument was undertaken in 1934 and 1964, but it was not enough. As a highly valued national symbol, the monument needed to be protected and preserved. In the late 1990s, a great effort was made to restore the Washington Monument to its former glory.

The restoration cost more than $9.4 million. It was sponsored by a partnership between government and private sources. Restoring the monument would take several years. During that time, chipped and patched stones were repaired and cracks were sealed where necessary.

New mortar replaced the old in many spots, and thousands of feet of interior walls were given a thorough cleaning. Some observation windows were resealed, and eight new warning lights were installed to protect aircraft as well as the monument from a collision. The heating and cooling systems as well as the elevators were improved. Other repairs to preserve the monument were also completed.

On February 22, 2002, a ceremony was held to celebrate both the completion of the restoration and the 270th anniversary of George Washington's birth. Maryland Representative Roscoe G. Bartlett spoke at the event. He noted that "George Washington was a giant among the many giants of our nation's founders and

To help celebrate the reopening of the monument in 2002, the Old Guard Fife and Drum Corps dressed in historic costumes and entertained visitors with music.

the single most **indispensable** individual responsible for America's success." With the restoration complete, the nation has shown that it still remembers and respects this great American. His monument once again stands as a worthy tribute to him.

Timeline: The Washington

1783	1799	1833	1836	1848	1854	1855

The Continental Congress proposes that a statue of George Washington on a horse be built.

George Washington dies.

The Washington National Monument Society is formed.

American-born architect Robert Mills wins the design contest sponsored by the Washington National Monument Society.

Work on the monument begins. The cornerstone is laid on July 4.

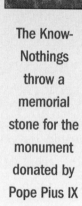

The Know-Nothings throw a memorial stone for the monument donated by Pope Pius IX into the Potomac River.

The Know-Nothings seize control of the Washington National Monument Society.

Monument

1861	1879	1880	1884	1885	1998–2000	2002
The Civil War breaks out, and work on the monument temporarily stops.	Construction on the monument resumes.	The monument's second cornerstone is laid on August 7.	The 3,300-pound (1,498-kg) marble capstone is placed on the monument on December 6.	The monument's formal dedication is held on February 21.	The monument undergoes an extensive renovation.	A ceremony is held to celebrate the completion of the restoration and the 270th anniversary of George Washington's birth.

INDEX

CREDITS

ARLINGTON NATIONAL CEMETERY
Photographs © 2005: AP/Wide World Photos: 2, 3, 4 left, 5 top, 7, 16 top, 19, 20; Cameramann International, Ltd.: 23 bottom; Corbis Images: 8 bottom, 8 left, 9, 10, 11 bottom, 14 top, 14 bottom, 15 bottom, 16 bottom, 17 bottom, 17 top, 18, 24 top, 25 top, 31 top (Bettmann), 25 bottom (Reuters/Bettmann), 1, 11 top, 13, 15 top, 21 bottom, 22 left, 28 (UPI); David J. Forbert: 5 right, 12 bottom, 12 top, 23 top; Dembinsky Photo Assoc./M. Kazmers/SharkSong: 27; Gene Ahrens: 4 bottom; Mae Scanlan: 21 top, 26 background, 30; Superstock, Inc.: 6 (P. Amranand), 29 (David Harvey), 22 right, 31 bottom (Jack Novak), 24 left.

THE CAPITOL
Photographs © 2005: AP/Wide World Photos: 46, 49, 55 bottom; Cameramann International, Ltd.: 33, 58 top, 59 bottom, 61; Corbis Images: 37, 40 top, 41 top, 42, 45, 51 top, 51 bottom, 52 bottom, 52 top, 55 top (Bettmann), 34 (Reuters/Bettmann), 47, 60, 63 bottom, 63 top (UPI/Bettmann); Library of Congress: 40 bottom, 41 bottom; North Wind Picture Archives: 39, 48 bottom, 48 top; Photri Inc.: 35, 38, 56, 57, 58 left, 58 bottom, 59 top, 62; Superstock, Inc.: 53; Tom Stack & Associates, Inc.: 54 (Jon Feingersh), 36 (Brian Parker).

ELLIS ISLAND
Photographs © 2005: AP/Wide World Photos: 104 bottom (Stephen Chernin), 71, 90, 91, 96, 97, 100; Corbis Images: 66, 67, 74, 78, 83, 88, 92, 98, 99, 101, 102, 103, 107 bottom left (Bettmann), 72 (Hulton-Deutsch Collection), 65, 104 top (Bill Ross), 70, 75; Eliot Cohen/Janelco Photographers: 86, 107 bottom right; Library of Congress: 79 (via SODA), 68, 69, 73, 80, 81, 82, 85, 93, 95, 106 top left, 106 top right, 106 bottom, 107 top; National Archives and Records Administration: 87; Statue of Liberty National Monument/National Park Service: 76, 77, 84, 89, 94, 107 center; Superstock, Inc.: 105.

★ ★ ★ ★

MOUNT RUSHMORE
Photographs © 2005: AP/Wide World Photos: 109, 121, 123, 126 bottom, 128, 129, 135 bottom, 136, 137, 139 bottom left; Dave G. Houser/Houser-Stock, Inc.: 113, 117; Greg Latza/PeopleScapes, Sioux Falls, SD: 110; National Park Service: 132 (Bell Studio), 126 top, 131 (Charles D'Emery), 119 (Reverend Carl Looke), 112, 118, 130, 139 bottom right, 139 top right (Rise Studio), 127 (Julian Spotts), 125, 134; North Wind Picture Archives: 116, 120 bottom; Root Resources/James Blank: 11; Stock Montage, Inc.: 120 top center, 120 top, 120 bottom center, 133, 135 top; Superstock, Inc.: 115, 122, 138.

THE STATUE OF LIBERTY
Photographs © 2005: AP/Wide World Photos/George Widman: 181; Corbis Images: 145, 164 (Bettmann), 141 (Joseph Sohm; ChromoSohm Inc.), 162 (Cathy Crawford), 178, 179, 182 top right (Jim Erickson), 143, 183 bottom right (Museum of the City of New York), 173 (Alan Schein), 154; Folio, Inc.: 144, 182 bottom (Jeff Greenberg), 147 left (Lelia Hendren); Free Library of Philadelphia: 160, 183 top left; Getty Images/Andrew Ward/Life File: 159 left; Hulton|Archive/Getty Images: 168; Library of Congress: 152, 153, 157, 163, 174, 175, 183 top right; Museum of the City of New York: 155; New York Public Library Picture Collection: 171; North Wind Picture Archives: 165, 172; NYC & Company: 180, 183 bottom left; Rigoberto Quinteros: 176; Statue of Liberty National Monument/National Park Service: 142, 146, 147 right, 149, 150, 151, 158, 159 right, 161, 167, 169, 170, 177, 182 top left; Yale University Art Gallery/Joseph Szaszfai: 148.

★　★　★　★

THE TOMB OF THE UNKNOWN SOLDIER
Photographs © 2005: AP/Wide World Photos: 200, 228 top right; Brown Brothers: 190; Corbis Images: 222, 223 (Bettmann), 220 (Wally McNamee), 191, 228 center (Medford Historical Society Collection), 203, 204, 210; Corbis Sygma/Bill Greenblatt: 214; Folio, Inc./Catherine Karnow: 195; Getty Images: 213, 229 top right (Tim Parker/Reuters), 192 (William Philpott/Reuters), 229 top left (Reuters), 187, 226 (Stefan Zaklin); Hulton/Archive/Getty Images: 196, 197 (Scott Swanson Collection), 198; Library of Congress/National Photo Company Collection: 202, 207, 208; National Park Service/Don Worth: 188, 228 top left; Photri Inc./T. Wachs: 186; Robertstock.com: 205 (W. Bertsch), 189 (D. Corson), 224, 228 bottom (D. Lada), 185 (J. Patton), 194 (H. Sutton); Superstock, Inc./Musee des Deux Guerres Explorer: 193; Time Life Pictures/Getty Images/Leonard McCombe: 211; U.S. Army Photo/Shannon Duckworth: 215, 229 bottom; Viesti Collection, Inc.: 219 (Richard Cummins), 216 (Joe Viesti).

THE VIETNAM MEMORIAL
Photographs © 2005: AP/Wide World Photos: 249 (Art Greenspon), 246 (Paul Sakuma), 250 (Schneider), 253, 255, 258, 263, 272 right, 273 left, 273 right (Charles Tasnadi), 266 (Nick Ut), 243; Corbis Images: 231, 260, 273 center (Bettmann), 265, 232 (Owen Franken), 256 (Catherine Karnow), 233, 271 (Joseph Sohm;ChromoSohm Inc.); Getty Images/Alex Wong/Newsmakers: 261; Hulton\Archive/Getty Images: 244, 245, 251, 268, 269; Magnum Photos: 240, 272 center (Leonard Freed), 234, 238, 239, 241, 242 (Philip J. Griffiths), 270 (Peter Marlow), 235, 237 (Marc Riboud); Stockphoto.com/Robert Ellison: 272 left; Vietnam Veterans Memorial Fund: 262 (Dan Arant), 248, 267.